1066 and Before All That

1066 and Before All That

The Battle of Hastings, Anglo-Saxon and Norman England

ED WEST

Skyhorse Publishing

Skyhorse Publishing books may be purchased in bulk at special discounts for sales promotion, corporate gifts, fund-raising, or educational purposes. Special editions can also be created to specifications. For details, contact the Special Sales Department, Skyhorse Publishing, 307 West 36th Street, 11th Floor, New York, NY 10018 or info@skyhorsepublishing.com.

Skyhorse® and Skyhorse Publishing® are registered trademarks of Skyhorse Publishing, Inc.®, a Delaware corporation.

Visit our website at www.skyhorsepublishing.com.

10 9 8 7 6 5 4 3 2 1

Library of Congress Cataloging-in-Publication Data is available on file.

Cover design by Rain Saukas

Paperback ISBN: 978-1-5107-7556-5
Ebook ISBN: 978-1-5107-1991-0

Printed in the United States of America

Contents

Introduction

In April 1066 an elderly, eccentric monk called Elmer noticed a shooting star in the sky from his Abbey of Malmesbury in Wiltshire. Seeing it as a bad omen, Elmer is supposed to have muttered: 'You've come, you source of tears to many mothers. It is long since I saw you; but as I see you now you are much more terrible, for I see you brandishing the downfall of my country.'

Few people reached old age in the eleventh century, but Elmer was one of them, and as a boy in September 989 he had seen the same 'hairy-tailed star' in the sky. Soon afterwards the Vikings had returned to England after almost a century, and so the comet's arrival now was not entirely welcome. Three months before the star reappeared King Edward had died, having first shouted wild and rather unhelpful prophecies about the country's destruction. During his long reign the slightly weird monarch had promised the throne to a number of very violent men, and the country was now in a state of deep foreboding even for the standards of the time.

The heavenly body, identified six centuries later by astronomer Edmund Halley, was indeed a bad omen, for 1066 would turn out to be a terrible year for England, with two invasions, three battles, and thousands of deaths. In the most famous of these clashes two armies of between seven and eight thousand men faced each other outside Hastings on October 14.

Elmer was lucky to have seen Halley's Comet a second time. Fifty years earlier the monk was so inspired by the Greek legend of Icarus that he built wings from willow trees and parchment, and proceeded to launch himself from the abbey's sixty-foot-high bell tower in a rather optimistic early attempt at manned flight. But even the fact that he broke both his legs and never walked again didn't dampen his cheery demeanour and enthusiasm (in fairness he did stay airborne for two hundred yards before crashing, or so he claimed).

Edward's successor King Harold II had a hell of a year since being proclaimed king in January. By the time of Hastings he had just spent a month marching an army two hundred miles up to the north of England, where his men had seen off another invasion from the flamboyant Viking maniac Harald Hardraada, before marching back again. Now he faced Duke William of Normandy, the humorless, hard-faced ruler of the most militaristic people in the known world, descendents of Vikings who had settled in France a century and a half before.

Few battles in history have had such catastrophic consequences for the losers, for as historian Elizabeth van Houts put it: 'No other event in western European history of the central Middle Ages can be compared for its shocking effects: the carnage on the battlefield, the loss of life and the consequent political upheaval.'

By the end of William the Conqueror's reign twenty-one years later, only two major English landowners were still in possession of their homes, one Englishman held a senior position in the Church, and just 5 percent of land was still owned by natives, while an entire class of five thousand *thegns*, England's aristocrats, had been killed, driven abroad or forced into serfdom or something similarly awful. In the worst instance of Norman violence over one hundred thousand people were killed in Yorkshire, an event known as the

'Harrying of the North' which left whole regions deserted for a century afterwards.

One-third of the entire country was set aside for royal forests, with large numbers of natives evicted from their homes that then became Norman pleasure gardens. Countless houses were demolished to make way for castles to enforce Norman authority, and the natives were collectively punished if any Norman was found dead in their neighborhood (while a Norman who killed an Englishman would go unpunished). The English language itself, which perhaps had the richest body of literature in western Europe at the time, would be suppressed for three centuries, by which time it would reemerge heavily influenced by the conquerors. Today, between a quarter and half of all words in the dictionary come from French, including almost everything to do with the law, government and war.

It's easy to cast the Normans as preeminent medieval bad guys, callous imperialists who oppressed everyone, stole their land, and forced them into serfdom. And on top of invading England, and later Wales and Ireland, they also had more conservative views about women and religion, and their approach to interfaith issues in the Middle East would not be entirely fashionable today. Indeed the word 'bigot' was originally a Parisian insult for Normans, and came from their habit of using the Germanic oath *'bei Gott'* or 'by God'.[1] They are also blamed for introducing the idea of feudalism, whereby most people were tied to the land and had to work for their master half the year in exchange for a penny or some dung.

In England, Norman ancestry has become synonymous with elitism, so that French-sounding names suggest privilege, while Anglo-Saxon ones appear humble. In the most popular British book and film series of recent years, the heroes have the very Anglo-Saxon sounding surnames Potter and Weasley, while the baddies go by the Normanesque Voldemort and Malfoy.[2] It's shorthand for humility versus entitlement.

The Normans sound like cartoon Hollywood upper-class English villains, blamed for creating long-standing class divisions, and to an extent this is true. To take one example, when Gerald Grosvenor, the multibillionaire 6th Duke of Westminster, was asked by a journalist what advice he'd give to a young entrepreneur hoping to become rich, he suggested 'make sure they have an ancestor who was a very good friend of William the Conqueror.'[3] Indeed the duke's forebear Hugh Lupus, 'le gros veneur' or chief huntsman, had been granted lands by William in the county of Cheshire in order to keep the Welsh under control. In the 1170s, his descendent Robert le Grosvenor had been given the manor of Budworth in the county, which is still home to the Grosvenor seat, the Eaton Estate. When, in 2016, the duke died, he left £8 billion ($10 billion) to his son.[4]

But, of course, the Normans weren't all bad. There were huge class divisions in English society in 1066, and feudalism was already in place;[5] the Godwin family, of whom Harold was head, were absurdly wealthy, possibly richer than his grasping successor. And, as well as building many beautiful cathedrals and castles, the Normans abolished slavery, maintained and improved Anglo-Saxon England's system of government, while their customs were in many ways more civilized. They tended to ransom their aristocratic opponents, while the English just killed them, which is partly why by 1066 the country had been worn down by several decades of feuding and murder.

And it all began when the last comet visited, and with the doings of an evil stepmother.

CHAPTER ONE

Red Sky at Night

Read any national history from this period, whether it's Ireland, Italy, Spain or even Egypt, and you'll find the Normans turning up at some point. And England made an awfully tempting target. By the mid-eleventh century, the country was one of the most prosperous in western Europe, with wool from the Cotswolds and East Anglia exported across the continent and a system of minting coins and collecting taxes that was way ahead of its rivals.

This was all quite impressive since only five hundred years earlier their ancestors had been illiterate raiders noted largely for the cruel deprivations they carried out on prisoners. The tribes known as the Angles, Saxons, and Jutes had crossed the North Sea from Germany and Denmark to Britain in the fifth century after the Romans left, conquering the south and east of the island. Converting to Christianity in the seventh century, the 'Garmans' (as natives called them) had gathered into a number of kingdoms that slowly absorbed each other until by the ninth century there were just four—Northumbria, Mercia, East Anglia and Wessex. However, at this point new barbarians from Scandinavia arrived, known to us as the Vikings ('raiders'), and in the 860s their armies overran three of the Anglo-Saxon kingdoms until in 871 just Wessex remained, ruled by a young, inexperienced and very neurotic king called Alfred. Against the odds, he fought off the invaders, and fifty years later his grandson Athelstan had conquered all of what is now England, roughly on its modern borders.[1]

England had become a rich and sophisticated state under the House of Wessex, culminating with the relative golden age of Alfred's great-grandson Edgar the Peaceful (959–975), who established full authority over the island's various warlords, despite being less than five feet tall. With peace came a huge growth in trade and learning, most of it done through the Church and its monasteries. The Angles and Saxons, despite being terrifying pagan barbarians to the Britons they conquered, had very quickly become devoted to Rome; partly, it has to be said, because they were so far away they didn't have to encounter the squalid reality of the place.

And so England in 1066 had law courts, counties, a tax system, and a very rich body of literature. Its people were in many ways more civilized than the Normans, who according to one contemporary 'found English prisoners well-dressed, long-haired and beautiful, much given to combing their locks—unlike the Normans' own shaven and crop-headed style.'[2] The English were 'a people greater, richer and older' than the Normans, according to Orderic Vitalis, a mixed Norman-English writer of the time.

The language, what we call Old English, had flourished in the century previously so that before the conquest some one thousand 'writers and copyists in English have been identified',[3] and, along with Irish, it was 'the most developed of Europe's vernaculars', with a literature far in advance of French.'[4] Much of this was owed to Alfred, who, as well as beating the Vikings, encouraged everyone to learn to read and also set up the *Anglo-Saxon Chronicle*, a series of books recording (the mostly depressing) events of the period written in five different locations.

King Alfred had built the first English cities since the Romans left, creating a system of 'burhs' that were fortresses where people could hide when the Vikings turned up, and these soon grew into towns. In the tenth century, London had property magnates for the first time—the Abbess of Barking, with twenty-eight apartments in the city, was the biggest. With peace, overseas trade increased, and England was connected to the global economy revolving around Pavia, northern Italy, through which goods from as far away as modern day Indonesia turned up in England.[6] A tourist trade sprang up in religious centres, centred around novelties such as Saint Swithun's relics in Winchester, although 'pilgrims' were often just merchants pretending to be on religious missions to avoid customs duties. Almost every big town in the country claimed to have some saint's remains, which could be very lucrative, and many were rather dubious; five different holy houses claimed to possess the head of Saint Oswald, so presumably at least four of them were wrong.

Largely thanks to King Alfred's literacy drive, as well as modern forensics, we know quite a lot about life in urban tenth-century England—and it was mostly grim. We know that hygiene was not of the highest standard, and that only monasteries had *neccessariums*, or toilets. We also know that the people suffered from parasites, the most sinister being the mawworm, a twelve-inch-long monster that sometimes popped out of the corner of people's eyes, *Alien*-style. The Anglo Saxons almost never washed, and remarked upon how strange it was that their Viking neighbours would comb their hair and bathe themselves (with soap made from conkers) before their Saturday night activities; it improved their chances with the ladies, observed one monk.

The weather must have made all of this even more unpleasant. England was far hotter in the tenth and eleventh centuries than it is now, with London enjoying the same climate as central France does today. There were almost forty vineyards in the south of Britain, spread as far north as Suffolk, not considered by wine buffs today as great grape country.

As for food, we know something of what the early English ate from a Latin vocabulary by Elfric, archbishop of Canterbury at the turn of the millennium, which discusses the roles played by the baker, ploughman, fisherman and shepherd. *Elfric's Colloquy* consists of a series of discussions between monastic master and young pupils designed to improve their conversational Latin, but it is also an insight into teaching methods and jobs.[7] It suggests that although the Anglo-Saxons kept pigs, goats and deer, they ate them rarely, as meat was expensive. Fish was more popular, although herring was also very costly. People mainly ate carrots, leeks, garlic, fennel and kale; kale was so popular that February was called *sproutkele* in Old English before the introduction of the Roman calendar.[8] In fact, the calendar was different to the one we have today in many ways. While January 1 was merely the day of Our Lord's circumcision, New Year's Day was on March 25, or Lady Day, a feast in honour of the Virgin Mary and her immaculate conception (nine months before Christmas). It is now called Mothering Sunday in Britain, or Mother's Day.[9] This calendar lasted until the seventeenth century, and may be the origin for the European custom of April Fool's Day, whereby people following the old system were laughed at.

Some ancient superstitions and bits of folklore survive from this era: 'If the sky reddens at nights, it foretells a clear day; if in the morning, it means bad weather,' goes the wisdom first written down by Bede in the eighth century; or 'Red sky at night, shepherd's delight', as people still say in England. Other bits of wisdom did not last so well, including one claiming that thunder on Wednesdays 'presages the death of idle and scandalous prostitutes'; you don't often hear people say that these days. Among the few other things a visitor to the tenth century might find familiar are noughts and crosses—the only game of the period that we still play.[10]

If you wanted to look after yourself, you could read the ninth century *Bald's Leechbook*, the first English medical guide, although it's not quite as medieval as it sounds, *laeceboc* meaning medicine book, rather than referring to leeches. Among the cures recommended was cutting the eyelid open to calm a swelling, treating a spider bite with crushed black snails and lower back pain with 'smoke of goat's hair'. It also suggests one might lash oneself with a whip made out of dolphin to cure insanity (at what point does someone doing this think 'my mental health is definitely improving'?) Alternatively, chicken soup was used as an ailment for sickness, and a thick, porridgey beer was drunk as much for its cleanliness (although most people did have access to clean water, at least outside of cities) as for its alcohol content, which was low by today's standards; still, a few pints would certainly dull reality. The *Leechbook* also deals with headaches, baldness, virility or lack of it, and 'talkative women and evil spirits', declaring: 'If a man be over-virile, boil water agrimony in Welsh ale; he is to drink it at night, fasting. If a man be insufficiently virile, boil the same herb in milk.'

There is lots of standard medieval gibberish: 'If a man's hair fall out, make him a salve; take great hellebore and viper's bugloss, and the lower part of burdock, and gentian . . . If hair fall out, boil the polypody fern, and foment the head with that very hot.'

It also suggests: 'Against a woman's chatter: eat a radish at night, while fasting; that day the chatter cannot harm you.' And, 'make this a salve against the race of elves, goblins and those women with whom the Devil copulates; take the female hop-plant, wormwood, betony, lupin, vervain, henbane, dittander, viper's bugloss, bilberry palants, cropleek, garlic, madder grains, corn cockle, fennel.'

Among the other folk remedies suggested at the time was drinking wolf's milk for problems in pregnancy and childbirth, or alternatively trying a dried and pounded hare's heart. For an epidemic of plague, take a 'hand of hammerwort' and some eggshell of clean honey and add some more herbs. Meanwhile, hearing troubles could be dealt with by pouring 'juice of green earthgall or juice of wormwood' into the ears. As for bladder problems, get some 'dwarf dwolse' and pound it, and then down it with two draughts of wine. You'll at least forget about your problems. For baldness, 'collect the juices of the wort called nasturtium' and rub a bit in.

We may laugh, but this was not especially irrational: before the scientific method and modern medicine in the late nineteenth century, most active medical treatment was more likely to kill you than make you better, so you could do worse than eating some herbs and hoping for the best. Anyone who actually thought himself knowledgeable about medicine was probably a menace and would just try making a hole in your head to see what happened.

But this is if you could get your hands on food, for starvation was a frequent event. *The Anglo-Saxon Chronicle* recorded grimly:

975 'Came a very great famine.'
976 'Here in this year was the great famine.'
1005 'Here in this year there was the great famine, such that no one ever remembered one so grim before.'

During the worst of these, a group of forty or fifty people were seen jumping off Beachy Head in Sussex while holding hands. And one of the oldest surviving English jokes says as much about their tragic lives as their humor.

Q: What makes bitter things sweet? A: Hunger.

Another Anglo-Saxon joke goes like this:

Q: What has two ears and one eye, two feet and 1,200 heads, one belly, one back, one pair of hands and one neck?

A: A one-eyed garlic seller with 1,200 heads of garlic.

You probably had to be there.

Almost every July the food ran out, and the poor would often feed themselves on ergot, the fungus that grows on rye bread and which in bad times was the only thing available. Unfortunately, this produces an effect similar to a bad acid trip, and medieval famines were probably not the best environments to experiment with recreational drugs; ergot-eaters would describe feeling anxious and dizzy, with a burning sensation in the arms and legs, strange noises in the ears, and uncontrollable twitching. A somewhat more enjoyable-sounding subsistence food of the time was 'Crazy Bread', a mixture that included poppies and hemp.

Life was often so bad that fathers would sell children younger than seven into slavery, and there was even a word in Old English for people who volunteered to give up their freedom, which at least ensured you got fed as a part of the livestock, since one man was worth eight oxen. Slaves, also called 'live money', still accounted for over 10 percent of the population by 1066, and 25 percent in more remote areas like Cornwall, so it wasn't quite the social democratic paradise that anti-Norman historians make out. In fact it was the Normans who phased out slavery, replacing it with the somewhat better condition of serfdom (which was still pretty awful, obviously).

Slaves were often poor people who had gone down in the world, or they were native Britons (or as the Saxons called them, 'Welsh', which means 'slave' as well as 'foreigner'), but sometimes they were there as a punishment, which was more practical than prison.[11] In the case of incest, the man convicted went to the king as his slave and the woman to the local bishop. Sleeping with another man's slave was also a crime: anyone who deflowered a virgin slave of the royal family had to pay fifty shillings, a huge sum; if she was a slave of the royal flour mill, it was half this amount, and for an underslave, the lowest class, only twelve shillings.

Bishop Wulfstan, a cleric and lawmaker at the turn of the millennium who was fond of delivering damning sermons on how everyone was going to hell, painted a grim picture of life when he slammed Englishmen who 'club together to buy a woman between them as a joint purchase, and practise foul sin with that one woman, one after another, just like dogs, who do not care about filth; and then sell God's creature for a price out of the country into the power of strangers.'

Even for free people poverty was the norm; the vast majority in 1066 lived in the countryside, which for most people before the

modern era meant a life of relentless toil and misery. It was also a
closed world, and unless they were forced into joining the army, or
fyrd,[12] most men would rarely even visit the next village, let alone
other parts of the country. People even two counties away might
speak incomprehensibly to them, and since violence was far more
common than it is today, a stranger would by law have to blow a
horn before entering a village to show he wasn't up to no good.[13]

Most free people were classified as *ceorls*, that is peasants, from
where we get the word 'churlish'. Dressed in the simple tunics worn
by most—there were no buttons at the time—they worked the land,
and often owned a small plot, although fields would not be enclosed
for centuries to come. The common meadow was ploughed in strips
of a 'furrow's length', or furlong, 22 yards wide and 220 yards long;
this would become the length of a cricket pitch as that game evolved
in the medieval countryside to become the quintessential sport for
the English man of leisure; furlong is also still a measurement used
in horse racing.

There were various different classes of peasant, each signifying
an extra gradation of misery and burden, such as the wonderfully
named *drengs* in the north of England, free peasants who only had
to give military service in exchange for land. Below them were the
lowly *geburas*, origin of the word 'boor', who had 'a formidable burden of rents and services'[14] and had to work two days a week for their
lord, plus three days a week during harvest and between Candlemas
(February 2) and Easter. A *gebura* also had to plough an acre a week
'between the first breaking-up of the soil after harvest [late August]
and Martinmas [November 11], and to fetch the seed for its sowing
from the lord's barn'. In total he had to labor on seven acres a year
for rent, on top of extra 'boon work', and also be a watchman from
time to time. In return for this he got ten pence a year at Michaelmas
[September 29], 23 bushels of barley and two hens at Martinmas,
and a sheep or two pence at Easter (two pence was obviously worth a
bit more back then). And they were relatively privileged; compared

to actual slaves, who could expect a punch in the face every Michaelmas if they were lucky, they were living the dream.

And shepherds got some perks in return for their two-days-a-week obligation, including twelve night's dung for Christmas. It might not sound like a great present from a twenty-first-century point of view, but they were happy (probably).

Above the *coerl* were the *thegn*, the Anglo-Saxon nobility, of whom there were about four to five thousand men. To be considered of this rank one had to own not just a relatively nice house and five hides of land, but also your own church; but even a *thegn*'s house wouldn't have been what one thinks of as a medieval pile, as most people lived in buildings made of wattle and daub, and it was only in the twelfth century when the wealthy began living in houses built of stone. The Romans had left large stone buildings, but many people considered them to have been a race of giants, and some actively avoided Roman ruins as they thought them haunted.

Even free men had certain duties towards their lords. Everyone was required to do physical labor and to take up arms. If the country was invaded, they would be required to join the *fyrd*, although most people would try to get out of this so that their crops didn't rot or something awful didn't happen to their women folk while they were away. It was this *fyrd* which was called in the summer of 1066 as the threat of foreign invasion materialized.

CHAPTER TWO

Ethelred the Unready

The origins of the disaster ultimately lie with the complicated love life of King Edgar. The great-grandson of Alfred the Great had come to the throne after his brother Eadwig had died at just nineteen; Eadwig had ruled for four years and was best remembered for missing his own coronation because he was in bed with a 'strumpet', and the strumpet's mother. Edgar was just sixteen when he became king and seems to have had a similarly active interest in the opposite sex. After his first wife died in 963 he carried off Wilfrida, a nun from Wilton Abbey, making her his mistress; as atonement for this the king was made to do penance for seven years by not wearing his crown and fasting twice a week, hardly a death-defying punishment (in fact now considered to be superb health advice and the basis of a fashionable diet).

However Wilfrida escaped from her convent and went back to her lover, and eventually they had a daughter, Edith,[1] although for whatever reason it didn't last and soon Edgar found love again. (Edith would later become a saint after a holy but short life). According to legend the widowed Edgar now heard about a young woman called Elfrida who was famously beautiful and so sent one of his noblemen, his foster brother Ethelwald of East Anglia, to go out to report on whether the story was true. Ethelwald found that she was indeed very beautiful and so married her himself. Edgar naturally wasn't too pleased about this, and came to visit, killing his love rival in a hunt and marrying Elfrida.

It wasn't the most auspicious of starts to a relationship, and Elfrida would later be accused of witchcraft, a power which supposedly allowed her to take the form of a horse. She was allegedly seen by a bishop 'running and leaping hither and thither with horses and showing herself shamelessly to them,'[2] although strangely no one else corroborated the bishop's story.

By now the last Viking-controlled areas of England had been absorbed, and under Edgar the country already had the basis of a legal system and a fixed currency, as well as counties that roughly correspond to today's.[3] However the smooth-running of the state depended on having a stable, healthy and not unhinged man on the throne, and Edgar alas died aged just thirty-one; the previous monarchs had passed away at nineteen, thirty-two and twenty-five, so he'd done relatively well to get that far. He left two sons by two different wives, one of his heirs violent and angry and the other meek but useless.

The crown passed to his elder son, Edward, who was aged only thirteen or at most sixteen. Edward was known for having uncontrollable rages and would strike fear into everyone around him and 'hounded them not only with tongue-lashings, but even with cruel beatings'[4], while his younger half brother, Elfrida's son Ethelred, 'seemed more gentle to everyone in word and deed'.

However Edward's reign didn't last very long, and ended as they tended to in this period, violently. After four years on the throne he was stabbed to death during a fight, after being dragged from his horse in a courtyard. No one's sure if it was premeditated, or as a result of a spontaneous brawl outside a royal residence (spontaneous brawls were frequent in medieval history). According to one unlikely story Elfrida[5] herself stabbed him, and the wicked stepmother immediately put her own son on the throne; he was apparently so ungrateful at having been made king that she hit him over the head with a candlestick. After this Ethelred was left with a phobia of can dles for the rest of his life, which must have been debilitating when it was the only source of artificial light.[6]

The *Anglo-Saxon Chronicle* said of Edward's murder that 'no worse deed than this for the English people was committed since they first came to Britain', and inevitably in death Edward 'the martyr' became more popular than he was in life. After an initial hasty burial, the former king was reinterred at Shaftesbury convent where a couple of unfortunate crippled peasants were apparently cured after visiting his remains; after some further miracles by his grave, he was dug up a second time and buried at the more prestigious abbey church.

His cult mainly grew because of the awfulness of his brother, hopelessly ineffective half the time and viciously brutal the rest. Ethelred became known as 'the Unready', literally 'badly-advised' in Old English, a pun on his name, which meant 'well-advised'. He is best remembered for paying the Vikings to go away in an enormous protection racket called Danegeld, and, as Rudyard Kipling wrote with the benefit of nine hundred year's hindsight, 'That you've only to pay 'em the Dane-geld, And then you'll get rid of the Dane!' Ethelred never did.

As well as the Danes, it was also a time of intense conflict within the realm. A chronicler called Byrhtferth wrote: 'Strife threw the kingdom into turmoil, moved shire against shire, family against family, prince against prince, caldormen against caldormen, drove bishop against the people and folk against the pastors set over them'.

Historians of the time are harsh to Ethelred. Apparently at his coronation Bishop Dunstan supposedly 'could not restrain himself, and poured out in a loud voice the spirit of the prophecy with which his own heart was full. "Inasmuch", he said, "as you aimed at the throne through the death of your own brother, now hear the word of the Lord. Thus saith the Lord God: the sin of your shameful mother and the sin of the men who shared in her wicked plot shall not be blotted out except by the shedding of much blood of your miserable subjects, and there shall come upon the people of England such evils as they have not suffered from the time when they came to England until then!"' It must have been very awkward.[7]

On the day Ethelred was crowned 'a bloody fire was seen in the sky', according to the *Chronicle*, signalling what a disaster he would be. Another incident from the start of his reign taken as a bad omen was the disaster which befell England's first and at the time only two-storey building, the royal house at Wiltshire, which collapsed during an assembled royal get-together, leaving only the local bishop standing in a Buster Keaton–style wreckage.

Hanging over the king was the cult of his murdered brother, which grew ever more popular during his reign, encouraged at every opportunity by Ethelred's enemies (that is, most people). The twelfth century chronicler William of Malmesbury said of Ethelred: 'the king was always ready for sleep and it was what he did best.' But his reign was also one of seedy and squalid murder, with a death toll in his court so high George RR Martin would balk at it. During his rule so many leading courtiers and noblemen were stabbed, blinded or hacked to death, with the king's permission or tacit agreement, that when a Danish pirate claimed the throne many Englishmen gave their support—and when you're losing in a popularity contest to a Viking you know you've really hit rock bottom.

The Vikings (again)

The first Viking onslaught, perhaps triggered by population pressure in Scandinavia and the invention of new sailing technology, hit Britain in AD 786 and accelerated with the 'Great Heathen Army' of 865. Large areas of eastern England had since been settled by Danes who had ruled semi-independently in York until the 950s— some 40 percent of villages in Yorkshire have Norse names so presumably there were a lot of them.

But Scandinavia continued to produce huge numbers of excess violent men to sail the seas, restlessly travelling the world to find new lands. In the east the Swedes settled along the rivers flowing down to the Black Sea where they created the first states in the region; the locals called them 'rowers' or *Rus*, and so their kingdom was named Kievan Rus, and later Russia. In the West, around the turn of the millennium Leif 'the Lucky' Ericsson became the first European to set foot in the Americas, a fact celebrated every October 9th on Leif Ericsson Day in the Scandinavian-dominated Upper Midwest states.[8]

Leif's father Erik the Red had also been an intrepid explorer who discovered Greenland, and on top of this seems to have been an all-round awful human being. Erik's own father had been exiled from Norway for a murder and Erik followed in his footsteps, forced to leave the country for 'some killings' and so heading to Iceland, which was where desperados at the time turned up. He then had to flee from the main settlement in Iceland after killing another man and afterwards once again from this more remote western colony where he murdered *yet another* three guys. He ended up in Greenland, a name he gave to attract settlers despite its most conspicuous characteristic being snow and ice (Iceland was already taken as a name and they could hardly call it Icierland).

However the Vikings by this stage were already being pacified, and the days when you could just merrily move house after murdering people were numbered — for Christianity was finally taking root. Even Erik's wife, the incomprehensibly named Thjodhildr, became a Christian and would not sleep with her husband until he abandoned the old gods, which was 'a great trial to his temper' apparently; their son Leif would also become a Christian. Since the time of Alfred the Great, when the Vikings were notorious for cruel and convoluted pagan torture rituals, the Danes and Norwegians had slowly embraced the new faith, although it hardly seemed to make them better behaved. What mainly happened is that the veneration of their goddess Frejya was adapted into worship of the

Virgin Mary, and the word Thor was replaced with Jesus on statues; other than that the religion's pacifism seems to have largely passed them by.

Driven out of England, the Vikings had also successfully established themselves in Ireland, which was hopelessly divided between countless different microkingdoms, although the Norwegians (whom the Irish called 'the fair foreigners') spent much of their time there fighting the Danes (known as 'the dark foreigners').[9] The Norwegian Vikings had established a number of cities there, chief among them Dublin in 988, which soon became the centre for their slave trade. Many Irish people were captured and sold off to the Middle East, while others were forcibly taken off to Iceland with Viking men; roughly half of Icelandic mDNA, which is passed through the female line, is Irish in origin.[10] The Dublin slave market was also where many unlucky English people would end up before being sold off to far flung places to live God-awful lives of misery.

During this period the Vikings travelled far, and many of their domains remained Scandinavian for some time. The Isle of Man, in between England, Ireland, Scotland and Wales, was Norwegian until 1266, and the island's parliament, the Tynwald (from *thing*, a Nordic council) is the oldest on earth. Likewise with the Orkneys and Shetlands, which had been heavily colonized by Norwegians and today use many Norse words in their dialect.

According to the thirteenth-century *Historiae Norwegia*, the Vikings wrestled control of the islands from their two indigenous inhabitants, the Picts and a mysterious group called the Pape. The Picts, the author thought, were only a bit taller than pygmies and they could do amazing things in the morning and evening but at midday they lost all their strength and hid in underground caves. The author also believed that the Pape were Africans who practised Judaism, so one can't be entirely confident in his primary sources.

The Scandinavian lands were also now forming into states. Norway had been united by a sort of semi-mythical king, Harold

Finehair, who got his nickname after he fell in love with a princess who would not marry him until he was king—so he vowed to not cut or comb his hair until he had done it. Finehair went on to have twenty sons, although that number was somewhat reduced by fratricidal killing.

Something of the reasonable Scandinavian character was already in evidence in the way that Christianity was introduced. In most societies once the monarch became Christian followers of the old religion were soon ruthlessly persecuted but only the Scandinavians had sought to make some sort of compromise. When Iceland voted to change religions it allowed pagans to continue to eat horse flesh and expose their children to the elements, like in the good old days.

Hakon the Good, king of Norway from 934, offended some countrymen because he wanted to chart a middle course over the pagan festival of Yul-tide honoring the old gods. The pagans wanted him to take part but, although as a Christian he couldn't, he didn't want to be too fanatical about it, and so instead inhaled the smoke from the boiling horse meat that had been sacrificed to pagan gods without eating it. When pressed he agreed to eat some of the horse's liver as a halfway measure. Luckily the controversy was eventually resolved when Hakon was killed by Erik the Red's sons over something else.

Viking leaders certainly didn't entirely abandon pagan ideas about sex, and Scandinavian rulers continued for some time the traditional practise of having a second sexual partner, called a *handfast* or 'Danish wife', who was not quite a second wife but neither exactly a mistress either. The Rus king St Vladimir, who acquired his halo after converting his people, had an exhausting seven wives and eight hundred concubines. Realising the Rus would have to adopt one of the Abrahamic faiths for political reasons, Vladimir chose Christianity over Islam largely because the latter prohibited alcohol, which was never going to sell well with the Russians.[11]

Their adventurers in Russia had brought the Vikings into contact with the Middle Eastern world. One Arab trader called Ahmad ibn Fadlan spent much time with the Rus, noting their tattoos, long hair, poor hygiene and general barbarism, including their music, of which he said: 'I have never heard anything more horrible than their singing. It is more like the barking of dogs only twice as beastly.'[12]

The Norse world was connected to the Islamic through the slave trade, and the rise and fall of Viking activity in England was linked to far away events. One theory is that the Viking revival of the 980s was affected by an African slave uprising in modern-day Iraq, in which black soldiers sided with the rebels, which resulted in the Muslim world wanting more European slaves instead.[13]

There were one or two cultural misunderstandings along the way; in one incident the Emir of Cordoba in Spain, Abd ar-Rahman II, sent an embassy to a Viking called Jorik of Denmark, which turned into something of a disaster. The Danes tried to make him bow but the Arab refused to, and eventually it ended with the visitor showing his backside to the king, who had tried to lower the entrance to force him to genuflect. The Viking queen also took a liking to the ambassador, a handsome poet called Yahya ibn Hakam al-Jayyani, which increased tension. Obviously the Viking fondness for eight-day-long drinking binges that ended in comas did not impress the Moors too much, although it was not entirely boorish as a society; the Vikings loved poems, or *scalds*, but they tended almost entirely to revolve around fighting.

Among the most important Scandinavian raiders was Olaf Tryggvason, nicknamed Crowbone because he was obsessed with reading omens (Viking leaders were often very superstitious, but being sea-borne raiders, their lives were directed by chance). His Swedish aristocrat mother Astrid was lucky to survive after Olaf's father was murdered by a rival, the sinister-named Greycloak, whose lackeys searched the countryside for the pregnant widow in order to kill her and her husband's heir. One version has them fleeing to Russia and being sold into slavery after they were intercepted by pirates. Then, reaching as low as he could get when he was exchanged for a single goat, Crowbone grew up as a farmhand in Estonia, before being discovered and freed by his uncle Sigurd. Now he became a great seafarer, and went on to own the largest Viking warship we know of, the hundred-foot Long Serpent, and also circumnavigated the British Isles; in 981 he turned up in Padstow in Cornwall.

Although the formation of Norway, Sweden and Denmark would ultimately lead to the pacification of Scandinavia, it also made these new Viking armies much larger and stronger than previous ones. And with a young and weak king on the throne of England, the Viking raids began again in the 980s, met by Ethelred with incompetence and cowardice.

Olaf Tryggvason was one of the leaders of a fleet of ninety-three longboats that attacked the east coast of England in the summer of 991, hoping to go from town to town demanding money. A force this big could devastate a huge area before any help could arrive, and people usually just gave the Vikings silver in the hope they would go away.

However after they turned up in Maldon, Essex, the local lord, Byrhtnoth, insisted on fighting them, despite being well into his sixties. When the Norsemen arrived at the shore and demanded money, the ageing warrior replied: 'We will pay you with spear points and sword blades.' This all sounds very heroic, but showing characteristic English fair play, Byrhtnoth refused to attack the Vikings while they were still on the causeway and agreed that they should be allowed to make their way ashore for a fair fight. The unsporting Vikings then slaughtered their English opponents. (Another explanation is that had the Vikings not been allowed over they would have just sailed away and he would rather engage them now when he was ready).

Although the old warrior died, along with some of his followers—many also ran off—he took a lot of Vikings with him, and the poem of *The Battle of Maldon* became an inspiring tale of English courage. It had an important national message, since Byrhtnoth's men came from across the country; while in reality England was disintegrating, and as the *Chronicle* recorded, no county would help the next. In the poem Byrhtnoth tells the Vikings:

> 'Listen, messenger! Take back this reply
> . . . that a noble earl and his troop stand here—
> guardians of the people, and of the country, the home
> of Ethelred, my prince—who will defend this land
> to the last ditch.'

Unfortunately the only copy of the poem was burned during a famous 1731 fire at the Ashburnham Museum in Westminster, along with half of all manuscripts from Anglo-Saxon England, and though the deputy keeper of the collection had just made a copy, which otherwise would have been lost, he hadn't got around to finishing the last fifty lines. So like someone who's borrowed a library book only to find out that the previous user has ripped out the last page, we'll never know how it ended. At any rate Byrhnoth died.

As a result of the battle and the subsequent raids, Ethelred paid Olaf £16,000 to leave, on condition that he convert to Christianity. That was a huge amount of money in those days (literally 16,000 pounds in silver), and naturally Olaf spent the rest of his very comfortable years very much loving Jesus. Olaf in fact forcibly converted large numbers of his subjects when he became king of Norway, maiming and torturing people who didn't embrace Christianity, which is perhaps slightly missing the point. Despite this, like many newly Christian Vikings, he maintained the custom of having two wives. However it didn't have a happy ending, and eventually he was killed in battle with a Norwegian rival, Earl Erik.

After Maldon Ethelred began the policy of paying off raiders, with at least £250,000 raised during his reign, with the money going up from £10,000 in 991 to £24,000 in 1002, £36,000 in 1007 and an astonishing £45,000 to £48,000 in 1012 alone. But the country could afford it, for at the time sterling was a valued currency accepted and imitated all over northern Europe (the word comes from *steor*, Latin for stable, at least according to one theory). England had seventy royal mints that produced the ten million coins that were at any one point in circulation, each of which was 92.5 percent silver. In recent years more of Ethelred's money has turned up in Scandinavia than in England.

And having seen Olaf come home with enormous sums of money, the other Vikings got the impression that England was a rich and cowardly country. Attacks continued in 993 with Bamburgh in Northumbria destroyed and 'much war-booty taken'. In 994 another Viking fleet arrived with a combined force of ninety-four warships and two thousand fighting men; that year London was successfully defended, and so the Vikings moved on to Essex, Kent, Sussex and Hampshire. In 997 Devon, Cornwall and Wales were assaulted and the following year Dorset and Isle of Wight got hit, while in 999 Norsemen landed in Rochester in Kent and defeated a local army.

The army in Kent fled in the face of superior numbers, because (according to the Peterborough version of the *Chronicle*) 'they did not have the help they should have had'. The *Canterbury Chronicle* recorded 'the ship-army achieved nothing, except the people's labor, and wasting money, and the emboldening of their enemies'. These were all none-too-subtle criticisms of the king, who had failed to provide any sort of leadership. On the one occasion, in 992, when Ethelred got all the leading nobles together to organize an army to fight the Vikings, the man he put in charge, Elfric, went and betrayed the secret to the enemy, for whatever reason. Afterwards, the king had Elfric's sons blinded.

In another one of his depressing sermons Wulfstan the Homilist noted English warriors watching helplessly while the Danes gang-raped their wives and daughters, while on another occasion a large group of townspeople did nothing while just three or four Vikings brought English people onto their boats for a life of slavery.

While England was powerless against the invaders, and with the millennium approaching, it seemed to confirm people's worst fears about the end of the world. The coming of the year 1000 was met with something approaching dread in some quarters, but Old English culture had a strong sense of doommongering at the best of times, which considering events was understandable.

Much of what we know of the Anglo-Saxons comes from their poetry, which would have been played around the fire of great halls accompanied by the six-stringed harp. Although only a handful of poems survive, they tell us something of their world, among them *Deor*, about a poet who has lost his position among a tribe called the Heodenings, and which recounts how the poet, or *scop*, was the living memory of the tribe. On a similar, depressing note, *The Wanderer* is about a man who loses his lord and is mournful, lamenting:

'The prudent man should under-
how ghastly it will be,
when all this world's wealth
shall stand waste,
as now divers.
over this mid-earth,
with wind shaken
walls stand,
with rime bedeck'd:
tottering the chambers,
disturbed are the joyous halls,
the powerful lie
of joy bereft,
the noble all have fall'n,
the proud ones by the wall.'

Probably not something you'd quote when volunteering for the Samaritans. Then there was *The Fortunes of Men*, dating to the late tenth century, which lists all the way people will die—crippled, falling from a tree, exiled, hanging and 'one a jabbering drunkard', which says something about the life quality of most people.

'Hunger will devour one, storm dismast another'
One will enjoy life without seeing light
One will have no choice but to chance
remote roads, to carry his own food and leave drew tracks among
foreign people in a dangerous land.'[14]

The poem concludes, however, that one will reach old age and a reasonable level of happiness; and everything in life, whether we are talented, good at throwing or clever, is all in God's hands, so there is no point worrying about it.[15] *The Fortunes of Men* comprises one part of the *Exeter Book*, a collection of ninety-six riddles still in the city's cathedral library where in 1072 it was given to the bishop. It is a precious record of early medieval England, although it has since been damaged, having been used down the years as a cheese board, breadboard and beer mat. Of the riddles, a dozen concern war, and some reflect ideas about the Christian faith, but most however describe everyday life with humor that is often quite lewd. One goes:

'I'm a wonderful thing, a joy to women,
to neighbors useful. I injure no one
who lives in a village save only my slayer.
I stand up high and steep over the bed;
underneath I'm shaggy. Sometimes ventures
a young and handsome peasant's daughter,
a maiden proud, to lay hold on me.
She seizes me, red, plunders my head,
fixes on me fast, feels straightway

what meeting me means when she thus approaches,
a curly-haired woman. Wet is that eye.'[16]

The answer is: an onion. The whole thing has a 1970s British sex
comedy feel to it. Another poem of the period goes:

'A youth came along to where he knew
she stood in a corner. Forth he strode,
a vigorous young man, lifted up her own
dress with his hands, thrust under her girdle
something stiff as she stood there'[17]

Anyway. The year 1000 did not mean the end of the world as
expected—in fact they had miscalculated Christ's birth by six
years—although the king's wife died soon afterwards, at which
point someone at the court came up with an ingenious plan of fighting off the Vikings by forming an alliance with a group called the
Normans. What could go wrong?

CHAPTER THREE

In Bed with the Normans

While England was being attacked in the ninth century the Dancs wcrc also launching raids on Francia, the former Roman province of Gaul which had been overrun by the Franks when the empire collapsed. The Franks were the most powerful of the barbarian German tribes and their king, Charlemagne, had in AD 800 been crowned 'Emperor of the West' by the pope; so started the complicated nonsensical entity called the 'Holy Roman Empire' which lasted, strangely, until Napoleon's time, and which no one—even at the time—understood. Charlemagne was behind what is called 'the Carolignian Rcnaissancc' which in csscncc bcgan the Middle Ages, introducing everything we associate with that period from Romanesque cathedral architecture to castles to Carolingian typeface. But his huge empire had no real coherence and only survived so long as there was a ruler as ruthless and strong as he was (which he was—Charlemagne killed something like fourty-five hundred Saxons[1] because they refused to convert to Christianity.) Charlemagne's grandsons, however, fell out and the war-torn country was left open to raids just as the Vikings were getting into their groove. One of the most serious was led by the semi-mythical Ragnar Lothbrook who attacked Paris in 851,[2] but they were especially menacing around the region formally known as Neustria, upriver from Paris, which contained lots of inlets and rivers, just the sort of places Vikings loved.

Following Alfred the Great's rise to power these raids in Francia got worse and in 912 a group of Vikings settled on the river Seine and decided that, whatever the French thought about the matter, they were staying. The Frankish king Charles the Simple, who despite his name was actually quite shrewd (the name might better be translated as 'honest') thought that it would make more sense to co-opt the Norsemen and use them to fight off other Vikings. He must have assumed the marauders' colony would collapse or be quickly absorbed—but as it turned out the Duchy of Normandy would become a monster that caused as much distress to France as it did to England.

It's common to refer to the Normans as 'French Vikings' but they weren't *that* Viking. In their culture and their military tactics the Normans by 1066 were rather like any other Franks; they hardly went near the sea, they fought on horses, spoke French, were deeply Christian and, like the Franks, were also moderate in their drinking compared to the English. Norman chroniclers were frequently disgusted by how much alcohol the English consumed, which is a criticism no Scandinavian would make. Say what you like about the Vikings, but they weren't sanctimonious.

Indeed the Normans aren't very Viking by ancestry; a 2015 study on people from the part of Normandy colonized by Norsemen showed just 15 percent had the blood group associated with Scandinavia, and none the specific markers linked to Norway.[3] Most likely the number of Viking settlers in France was small.

These Norsemen were led by Hrolf or Rolf—Rollo in French— who agreed to Charles's terms. However according to one slightly unlikely story, Rollo refused to bow to anyone, so when it came time to kiss the Frankish king's feet during the agreement he got one of his sidekicks to do it, but the big lumbering man upended Charles because he didn't want to bow either.

Charles made his daughter Gisla marry Rollo, who promised to become a Christian in that vague way Vikings tended to without really meaning it. Apparently Rollo made gifts to churches, but also organized pagan human sacrifices, which is called hedging your bets.[4]

However Gisla died childless and Rollo then reinstated his mistress Poppa; their son William Longsword succeeded him and helped the colony to survive and thrive. The early settlers had smashed up most of the monasteries in the region, but as their colony became known as Normandy ('land of the North-men') these Normans turned into the most faithful, indeed deranged, Christians.

And though a century later the Normans spoke French, they still had some connections to Scandinavia and were allowing their friends from the old country to use Normandy as a base for attacks on England. This was extremely damaging, and at one point Ethelred may have tried invading Normandy, but the mission was aborted in failure, as his plans tended to be. So instead, after Ethelred's wife Elfgifu died, the thirty-year-old king decided to get the Normans onside by marrying the twelve-year-old Norman princess Emma, daughter of Duke Richard. Confusingly, and weirdly, Ethelred didn't like the name Emma and preferred to call her Elfgifu—which she must have loved. It wasn't to be a happy marriage, and the conniving queen showed nothing but contempt for her husband throughout their unhappy union.

Emma came from a long line of unconventional marriages, as Normans had not entirely rid themselves of the old Viking custom of polygamy. Rollo's son William, before being murdered by the Count of Flanders, had had both a wife and a mistress, but like his father had only produced children with the latter. (His former wife Luitgarde did have three children with her second husband, the wonderfully named Theobald the Trickster.)

The same pattern occurred with Emma's father, Duke Richard the Fearless. Emma's mother Gunnor apparently met Richard when he spotted her sister out on a hunting expedition; the sister wasn't interested so sent Gunnor to his bed when he turned up at her home. It all ended happily, more or less, despite the fact that Richard was already married to a French princess.

Gunnor, like any good Norman woman, was devout and donated land to the local monastery at Mont Saint-Michel;[5] a friendly monk called Dudo said she was 'well versed in the talents of feminine artistry', whatever that meant. Another, called Warner, celebrated her in a poem which also includes a degenerate Irish priest called Moriuht, who despite sexual escapades with nuns, widows and even boys comes to court seeking the help of Countess Gunnor.[6] In the poem Moriuht is dressed in rather unappealing fashion: 'in front of his buttocks he wore a black covering of a goat . . . and his genitals were visible in their entirety and the black hairs of his arse and groin. In addition, his anus . . . constantly gaped so openly whenever he bent his head and looked down on the ground, that a cat could enter into it and rest (there) for an entire year'. The countess, despite his appearance, agrees to his pleading and helps Moriuht rescue his wife.

Emma ended up as the wife of two kings of England, the mother of another two, and the step-mother of two more, but her marriage to Ethelred would be one of the more disastrous foreign policy mistakes in English history.

The young Norman princess arrived in England in the spring of 1002 during a period of intense Viking activity. She was in her early teens, her husband was twenty years older, and had at least ten children already, some of whom were fully grown men. The two families distrusted each other, Emma was unpopular for being French, and it was made worse when a French follower of hers betrayed the city of Exeter to the Vikings; why he did this, or whether Emma was at all to blame, we can never know, but it set things off to a bad start.

Although the Normans were themselves a bit rough around the edges, Emma may have got some idea of the violent nature of English politics when just before her wedding the ealdorman of Essex made a deal to pay off some Vikings but got into an argument with the king's high-reeve about it and killed him in a rage. The Essex man was banished from the kingdom.

She and her husband came to utterly despise each other, and Ethelred 'was so offensive even to his own wife that he would hardly deign to let her sleep with him, but brought the royal majesty into disrepute by tumbling with concubines'.[7]

Sweyn Forkbeard

That same year, and after a decade of inaction, Ethelred lost his patience and on November 13 ordered the murder of Danish settlers in England, a notorious event known as the 'St Brice's Day Massacre'. He was recorded as saying. 'A decree was sent out by me with the counsel of my leading men and magnates, to the effect that all the Danes who had sprung up in this island, sprouting like weeds amongst the wheat, were to be a destroyed by a most just extermination'.

Although the order was probably just for men to be killed, and maybe only Danish mercenaries who had previously worked for Ethelred, some reports claim that women and children were also murdered, and in the worst incident the Danes in Oxford were apparently all burned to death inside the church of St Frideswide where they'd sought refuge. Local legend says that captured Danes were skinned alive and that the doors of churches were made with their skins, after they had been flayed to death, although tests on eleventh-century church doors showed them to be made from regular cattle skin, so that was probably just a story people told children to scare them. However in 2011 under St John's College in Oxford the remains of thirty-nine males were discovered, most likely Danes hacked to death, and forensics showed that the victims had been running away from their attackers when they were cut down.[8] However appalling the massacre was, it was also foolish, as it provoked a response from a very violent Viking called Sweyn Forkbeard, who was also king of Denmark.

Sweyn had become ruler after overthrowing his own father, Harald Bluetooth, in the 980s. The country had only recently been united, by Sweyn's grandfather Gorm the Old, described by German chronicler Adam of Bremen as a 'savage worm' who tortured Christian missionaries to death. Gorm was a firm character, by all accounts, but a loving husband; he built a series of stones with runic inscriptions for his wife when she died, called the Jelling Stones, still in existence. (All the worst figures from this period tended to be faithful, loving husbands.)

Gorm's son Harald, whose nickname probably reflects his terrible dentistry, made his father turn in his grave by becoming a Christian—quite literally.[9] Bluetooth joined the faith in AD 960 for a typically Viking reason, after a priest called Poppo held a red-hot poker in his hands without burning himself. Poppo had courageously (or stupidly) told the Vikings that they were worshipping demons, and was challenged to carry the incredibly hot iron a number of paces before dropping it. Afterwards he apparently had clean wounds. After decades in which Christian missionaries had made no headway in Scandinavia by making theological arguments about love and peace, this impressed the king no end. Harald was so keen on the new religion he actually converted his father to Christianity, even though Old Gorm was technically dead, and had him reburied in a new church he had built.

Sweyn had raided England previously, and had already conquered Norway in a battle in which Olaf Tryggvason was killed, drowning in his armor after jumping out of the Long Serpent. (Sweyn and his Norwegian allies had turned up to the battle with 130 ships, Olaf with just 11, and this brought an end to his campaign of rather aggressive Christian evangelism.) Now Sweyn's sister Gunnhild was among those killed on St Brice's Day, or so he claimed, and he used this as a pretext to start raiding—although, to be fair, it's not like he needed one. Gunnhild was by some accounts the wife of Pallig, a Viking who had worked for Ethelred but double-crossed him; before being murdered Gunnhild had had to watch her husband Pallig being executed too.

The man responsible for her death was a Mercian nobleman called Eadric 'Streona', his nickname meaning 'the grabber', a particularly seedy character who turns up in various accounts stabbing someone in the back, both metaphorically and literally. He's such an archetypal, irredeemable baddie it's hard to believe everything that was written about him; barely a year seemed to go by without Eadric murdering or blinding someone.

But Streona was just the most extreme example of the terrible, bloody courtiers who surrounded the king, both malignant and incompetent, and Ethelred's judgment only got worse as he got older. In 1005 two of his advisers died, which further damaged the king's ability to run the country; another was brought down because of 'unjust judgements and arrogant deeds' while a nobleman called Aeflhelm was killed and his two sons blinded by Eadric Streona after Eadric had offered him hospitality, about the worst crime that could be committed at the time. Eadric was also married to Ethelred's daughter, which complicated things.

The Vikings did leave England alone in 1005, but only because there was a massive famine. The following year Sweyn Forkbeard was back and again in 1007, and this led to another huge bribe and peace for two years. The attack in 1006 is noteworthy only in that the Danish army ravaged the south of England, and attacked a meeting place of the Wiltshire militia with the slightly amusing name of Cuckamsley Knob.

It didn't help that the English court seemed to be almost comically divided between different factions from the old kingdoms of Wessex and Mercia, which led in 1005–1006 to a court coup, led by the Mercian Streona. The year 1007 was especially humiliating, with Ethelred paying out £30,000 in Danegeld while Sweyn swanned around the south of England, parading outside the capital Winchester in full view of its terrified inhabitants, while Ethelred hid in faraway Shropshire.

Under reforms initiated by King Ethelred every 310 hides of land had to provide enough money to construct a warship, and every eight hides was to provide armor for a single soldier. By 1009 Ethelred had raised enough for eighty ships, the largest navy ever seen in England, a spectacular feat that went amiss when the entire armada mutinied. The English navy ended up fighting itself off the Hampshire coast, destroying a third of their own fleet even before the Vikings arrived; not textbook leadership by any means. It was caused by a dispute over who was in charge: Streona's brother Brihtric, leader of the Mercian faction at court, accused Wulfnoth, head of the West Saxon clique, of piracy. Wulfnoth 'seduced the crews of twenty ships from their allegiance' and then went off and conducted raids against the south coast. Brihtric and his Mercians chased them but were mostly destroyed in a storm.

Running out of ideas, in 1012 the king officially launched the *heregeld*, army tax, also called *gafol* ('tribute'), or as it became popularly known, *Danegeld*, formalizing what had been practise since he'd paid off Olaf. Danegeld was Europe's first nationwide, official tax since Roman times, and lasted until 1161, despite the fact that by then the Vikings had last appeared a century before. Much of it was used to pay one load of Danes money to fight off some other Danes, because no one could properly organize and lead an army.

The following year Sweyn launched a full-on invasion of England, according to one account fearing that Ethelred might attack Denmark, although what gave him the idea the English king could successfully pull this off is anyone's guess. He sailed up the Humber, while another terrifying Norseman, Thorkell the Tall, arrived in the southeast and sacked Canterbury. Thorkell was one of a new breed of *Jomsvikings,* or 'super-vikings', who were a sort of order of knights that predated Crusades-era groups such as the Knights Templar, but with probably less emphasis on chivalry and saving fair maidens and more on violence.

As Thorkell's men were plundering and burning their way through the south of England the king issued an edict ordering three days of prayer. Only bread, herbs and water were to be eaten, and everybody had to walk barefoot to church 'without gold or ornaments'. The edict, issued in every church, ended with 'God help us, Amen'—which rather sounds about as reassuring as a pilot telling everyone not to panic.[10] Meanwhile Bishop Wulfstan introduced Sunday trading laws banning shops from opening in the hope it might persuade the Almighty to get onside.

In Canterbury, Thorkell and his gang of super-vikings kidnapped the archbishop, the unfortunate Aelfeah. After several months of imprisonment some drunken members of the gang pelted him to death with cattle bones, and Thorkell, who had agreed to baptism that very morning, was so disgusted by this behavior that he switched sides. (Ethelred also gave him a huge pile of cash, which might have encouraged his conscience to make the right choice.)

Meanwhile the heavily Danish northern and eastern parts of England had submitted to Sweyn. He took his army on to Oxford, Winchester and Bath, and within a year all of the country accepted him as king. Ethelred had lost so much support that the nation was prepared to give the Danes a shot at running the place. The main selling point of having a Viking running the country is that at least they're good at stopping other Vikings coming here.

Among the first to submit to Sweyn was Uhtred the Bold, ealdorman of Northumbria[11] and Ethelred's own son-in-law (he was married to the king's daughter, yet another Elfgifu). Meanwhile the daughter of Aelfhem, a nobleman who had been murdered by Eadric Streona, was married to Sweyn's son Cnut, or Canute—just to confuse things she was called Elfgifu as well. Ethelred's policy of murdering court rivals was showing itself to be surprisingly divisive.

Cementing his historical reputation as a cowardly, weasel-like figure, Ethelred fled the country for Normandy and it was left to his son Edmund 'Ironside', to lead the fight against the Danes. Edmund, made of stronger stuff than his father, showed enough mettle to make Sweyn leave the country with a number of hostages. Five weeks later Sweyn dropped dead, described by *Anglo-Saxon Chronicles* as a 'happy event'.[12] Now Viking leaders in Gainsborough pledged their allegiance to Canute, who was just eighteen years old,[13] but the ruling clique further south now sent for Ethelred in Normandy, and the king returned and marched on Canute's force in Lincolnshire.

Even now the noblemen were reluctant to take Ethelred back. The old king formally agreed to a list of conditions, in which he promised to rule the country better, the first known contract between king and subjects in English history. The 1014 agreement with Ethelred included the declaration by the nobility that 'no lord was dearer to them than their rightful lord, if only he would govern his kingdom more justly than he had done in the past', which showed they weren't entirely confident in his abilities.

Ethelred still had to contend with Danes occupying London Bridge, but one of his new allies, a young Norwegian called Olaf the Fat, had an idea. It might seem strange that Vikings were defending London, but the second round of Norse invasions are more complicated because a lot of Scandinavians were now fighting on the side of the English. The most fierce resistance to Sweyn's invasion came from Danes in East Anglia, led by Ulfkell Snilling, an Anglo-Danish leader in Norwich who was so powerful the region was sometimes referred to as 'Ulfkell's Land'. Olaf was the great-great-grandson of Harold Finehair, and he would incongruously became a saint later after a lifetime of violence. At the time, though, he was barely eighteen and unusually strong. As the Norse chronicle *Heimskringla* records, the Danes had at this point a fortress at Suthvirki—Southwark—and held the bridge, with Olaf's men north of the river in London itself but besieged by more Danes. With it looking like the Danes on both sides would link up with those on the bridge, Olaf volunteered to lead a river assault on the bridge, using longboats covered with wicker and green planks that were resistant to fire.

Olaf attached cables around the wooden pilings of the bridge then secured the cables to his ships downriver, all the while being pelted with rocks and spears. The old wooden bridge collapsed and the Danes drowned, while the Norwegians and English were able to land on an undefended position on the south bank and take back Southwark.

There is still a St Olaf Stairs marking the spot where the enormously strong Viking tore down the bridge, and the battle is still recalled in playgrounds. *The Saga of Olaf Haraldson*, a Norwegian epic poem from the thirteenth century, includes a song with the lyrics, 'London Bridge is broken down, Gold is won, and bright renown,' and by the seventeenth century the current version, *London Bridge is Falling Down*, was heard sung in England.[14] Olaf later became a saint, despite being 'slightly addicted to concubines' throughout his reign—but hey, nobody's perfect!

Even with this victory, it was a deeply depressing time for the country. That same year, 1014, Bishop Wullstan wrote his *Sermo Lupi ad Anglos*, 'The Sermon of the Wolf to the English', in which he blamed the sins of the people for their woes, among them 'murderers and whores' and 'foul fornicating adulterers'.[15] Wulfstan, an archbishop of York known as 'Lupus' (i.e. wolf) to distinguish him from an earlier namesake, was fond of quite fiery sermons. When the Vikings began turning up Wulfstan declared: 'It is written and was long ago prophesised, "after a thousand years will Satan be unbound". A thousand years and more is now gone since Christ was among men in a human family, and Satan's bonds are now indeed slipped, and Antichrist's time is now close at hand.' Wulfstan must have been great fun to be around.

And despite the victory in London things soon went wrong. Ethelred's eldest son Athelstan died in June 1014; then in September England suffered its worst flooding in living memory.

Ethelred organized a conference in which all would be forgiven if the English united to face the threat of renewed Viking attacks. However he and his clique just couldn't help themselves and there were further vicious murders in 1015 when the northern thegns Sigeferth and Morcar were killed through the treachery of Eadric and the king. Ethelred then seized their property and Sigeferth's widow Ealdgyth was taken to the Abbey at Malmesbury. However Edmund Ironside rose in rebellion against his father, seized the north of England and married Ealdgyth.

Ethelred's health was failing—it was quite a stressful job—and in April 1016 he died during another Danish attack on London, and was buried in St Paul's Cathedral. He's generally remembered as one of the worst kings to ever rule England, although his reign was also not without its artistic moments, with plenty of manuscripts dating from the period, among them a version of *Beowulf* and the *Exeter Book*, and a number of monasteries founded. Although most of this had nothing to do with the badly advised king.

The king did leave one important legacy; in 997, the *Chronicle* record, 'Ethelred ordered the shire reeve and the twelve leading magnates in each locality to swear to accuse no innocent man, nor conceal any guilty one'. This was the earliest record of a 'jury of presentment', or as it later became known, a Grand Jury. This may have been an older custom in the east of England, possibly a Scandinavian tradition, but Ethelred made it formal, and the Grand Jury is still part of the legal system in the United States today, although it was dropped in England itself in 1933—so in the final scheme of things lawyers have made a lot more from him than the Vikings ever did.

CHAPTER FOUR

King Canute and the Waves

After Sweyn's death, his then eighteen-year-old son Canute had landed in Sandwich to return his father's hostages—minus their hands, ears and noses (although more sympathetic accounts say this is all black propaganda and he only slit their noses open). After this the young man was at a loose end: his elder brother Harald had been given Denmark and Canute spent two years wandering around the North Sea with ten thousand Danish soldiers in perhaps the largest, longest and bloodiest gap year in history.

Now that Ethelred was dead Canute arrived in England with 160 ships, and much of the country accepted him as king, presumably feeling that the country needed a strong leader who didn't mind cutting off a few body parts. Many English noblemen, judging by the names of those who did homage, also supported the excitable young man, although it wasn't all plain sailing; when Uhtred of Northumbria surrendered he was murdered by Canute's men.

Meanwhile Edmund had the support of the Witan, or Witenagemot, literally 'wise men meeting', the Anglo-Saxon ruling council whose main job was to choose the king. In some tenuous ways a precursor to Parliament, it was the oldest English government body, a feature in Anglo-Saxon kingdoms perhaps as far back as the seventh century or even back to their time on the continent, although some historians think this is all romantic Victorian nonsense dreamt up to show how brilliant England has always been. Whatever the Witan actually did, it was abolished by the Normans.[1]

Although Canute sometimes resembles a violent psychotic maniac, Edmund Ironside was no shrinking violet either—he once threw a spear at Eadric Streona, and his throw was so powerful that the weapon bounced off Eadric's shield and went through two men beside him. Eadric certainly deserved it.

When the Danes arrived with 160 ships Eadric changed sides and took 40 boats with him, offering his help to Canute. Later in 1016 when Edmund seemed to be winning, Eadric changed again. Then the two sides met in a decisive battle, at Assandun in Essex, in which Edmund lost; little is known about the fight except that the bishop of Dorchester was killed while saying Mass, while an abbot also died in battle (it wasn't unknown for priests to fight at the time).

Afterwards Eadric changed sides once again, back to Canute.

And following months of fighting, Edmund agreed to joint rule with the Dane. It was Eadric, of all people, who managed to get them to meet by the River Severn in Gloucestershire, where they swapped hostages and partitioned the country. However, this was the early medieval period and no story is complete without a mysterious, untimely death. In November Edmund expired, and rumors abounded that either Canute's supporters or Eadric had killed him in some awful way. Henry of Huntingdon, a twelfth-century historian, said Eadric murdered Edmund while 'concealed in the pit', i.e. a toilet; when Edmund retired there 'for the purpose of easing nature' he was stabbed in the backside by the treacherous nobleman. One Norman historian claimed that Eadric invented a sort of crossbow which struck Edmund 'in the fundament' and 'went up as far as the lungs' without leaving a trace;[2] which seems rather out of the reach of the technology of the time.[3]

Now sole ruler, Canute immediately followed the Viking tradition of marrying his defeated enemy's wife, Emma of Normandy, despite already being married to yet another Elfgifu. To add to Ethelred's lowly standing in history, Emma was devoted to Canute, in contrast to the complete contempt and disgust she felt for her first husband.

In her officially commissioned biography, modestly titled *In Praise of Queen Emma*, written many years later, Ethelred's former queen presents Canute, ten years her junior, as a dashing young Scandinavian sex machine. The book describes his invasion fleet as the stuff of erotic fiction: 'For if at any time the sun cast the splendour of its rays among them, the flashing of arms shone in one place, in another the flame of suspended shields'. It's true to say that the best Viking ships, the *drekkars* or 'dragons', were elaborately colored with dragon imagery and a fleet must have been a sight. While Danish men, covered in jewels and elaborate and large brooches, with gold rings on their fingers and ostentatious buckles fastening their tunics, must have looked quite dashing, in a vulgar *nouveau-riche*-Russian-mafia sort of way.

Emma's book also makes Canute's pursuit of her sound more romantic than it probably was. Apparently the Viking sent out search parties to find a noble woman and 'obtain her hand lawfully' but eventually they located 'the most distinguished of the women of her time for delightful beauty and wisdom'—Emma. It sort of suggests she was wooed, when Vikings didn't really do 'wooing', as such. The *Chronicle* only record that Canute ordered Emma 'to be fetched as his wife'. In contrast, *In Praise of Queen Emma* doesn't even mention her first husband Ethelred, a bit of a glaring omission for a memoir.

The Danish conquest of 1016 and the Norman conquest half a century later had much in common, although in Canute's case he started off ruthless and then mellowed, while William the Conqueror began in a conciliatory way and progressively got more unpleasant. To start with, Canute ruthlessly murdered a number of opponents, among them four of the leading native noblemen, but Canute was fair-minded in his own way: he soon had Eadric executed for betraying his own people for Canute. Emma's book is gleeful when discussing Eadric's death; according to her account Streona came to Canute and demanded payment for his help in betraying Edmund, and so Canute told a Norwegian called Eric: 'Pay this man what we owe him: that is to say, kill him.'

Henry of Huntingdon recalls that Eadric told Canute he'd killed Edmund, to which the Dane replied 'for this deed I will exalt you, as it merits, higher than all the nobles in England' and then had him decapitated and his head stuck on the Tower of London (which didn't exist then, which slightly ruins the story). The *Chronicle* simply stated that Eadric was 'slain . . . very rightly'. In contrast Emma's biographer said Canute was lenient to those who had been loyal to his enemy, for he 'loved those whom he heard to have fought previously for Edmund faithfully and without deceit'.

Canute's first act was to raise £82,000 of Danegeld, which he awarded to himself, giving most of it to his own army on condition that they head home, adding a crucial ingredient that Ethelred missed—threatening extreme violence if they returned.

A Viking ruled England for the first time, but though a bloodthirsty killer in his youth, the new king also became a fanatical Christian. In 1023 he held a national ceremony of reconciliation, having Archbishop Aelfeah's remains taken from London to Canterbury behind a procession of both groups. The body of the martyred archbishop had become a focus of anti-Danish sentiment so he wanted it out of the way of London (whatever Canute's religious beliefs, there was always an ulterior motive for everything he did).

The king was very fond of great showy events like these; after Edmund's death Canute visited his grave in Glastonbury and referred to him as his 'brother', a somewhat two-faced gesture considering he'd had Edmund's actual brother Edwig murdered in 1017. By now all of Ethelred's male heirs by his previous wife were dead, except the children of Edmund Ironside, two very young boys called Edward and Edmund. Canute had them sent to his half brother Olof in Sweden with the order to have them quietly killed, but Olof took pity on them and secretly sent the boys off to Hungary, which was sufficiently far out of Canute's reaches.

Canute ruled harshly, and this made him tremendously popular. He held a meeting in Oxford where both Englishmen and Danes accepted the laws of King Edgar, and this became a legal code that all subjects, whatever nationality, had to obey. Under Canute a Danish community flourished in London. There was a Densemanestret in the Strand and a Denscheman parish in Westminster, both with churches of St Clement of the Danes.[4] He divided England into four parts, largely handing it out to his friends,[5] and lots of Danes became quite rich; men such as Hakon, **Hrani** and Eilifr were made *jarls*, a Scandinavian title that became the English 'earl'. This replaced the older Saxon title of ealdorman, (although alderman remained as a position in local government until abolished in 1973). Canute also appointed a series of local governors, or reeves, in each county, who came to be called *shire-reeves*, or sheriffs; today their role in England is largely ceremonial and consists of putting on an ostrich feather hat once a year to greet the Queen, but the eleventh-century position of sheriff was much closer to the Wild West idea—you got to ride around on a horse and occasionally kill bad guys.

Today Canute is known as 'Knut the Great' in Scandinavia, but in England he is best remembered for an incident in 1023 when he tried to push back the waves at Southampton, apparently under the illusion that being the most important politician in Scandinavia made him able to control the sea. In Canute's defence, he was only trying to prove to sycophantic courtiers that he was merely a man, with the words: 'Let it be known to all people that the power of kings is empty and weak. Only one person is fit to be called king. That is the Lord God who is obeyed by heaven, by earth and by the sea!'

But the story became twisted, probably by gormless peasants who missed the point and told their friends they'd heard the Danish king shouting at the sea. The moral of the story is—never try to be clever, as most people are too stupid to get it.

Still, if you do go around chopping people's ears off, don't be too surprised if you end up surrounded by sycophants. The story only emerged about a century later so it's hard to tell how much store should be put on it, or why it would become well-known; one would think that for the average person living in Canute's reign the story about him cutting off all the hands and feet of hostages would be more memorable.

After the Southampton incident Canute stopped wearing the crown altogether, placing it on a statue of Christ which he kept in his court; while he even paid for the shrine of the East Anglian king St Edmund in Bury as a belated apology for his ancestors' uncouth behaviour. (Edmund had suggested to some marauding Vikings they think about welcoming Jesus into their lives and to cut a long story short, they said no.) The king also gave generously to the Church and in later life visited Rome in the hope that the Almighty might overlook all those murders he committed.

The Danish King also ordered the destruction of all pagan idols, and eventually banned polygamy, so that under Canute's law, 'Foreigners, if they will not regularize their marriages are to depart from the land with their goods and their sins'. This was done to protect the peoples' souls 'from hell-fire', and would be fine if it weren't for the fact that Canute had two wives and he was a foreigner. In fact he became something of a religious fanatic, outlawing labor of any kind on a Sunday; and if a slave was forced to work by his master on the Sabbath he would be freed. Canute also ruled that if a man commits fornication (sex outside marriage) with a woman he is to be condemned, but if a woman commits it she is to become 'a public disgrace, and her lawful husband is to have all that she owned . . . and she is to forfeit her nose and ears'. The law also stated that people should 'love king Cnut with true fidelity'. Or else.

But Canute was laid-back and Scandinavian when it came to his own sexual needs. Most kings had mistresses, but Canute continued the Danish tradition of having a chief mistress, a *handfast*. So instead of divorcing Elfgifu when he became king and married Emma, he sent her off to Denmark to be his queen there with their young sons Sweyn and Harold, while Emma stayed in England. The two families did not get on, and in her autobiography, Emma only mentions in brief that, 'It was said that the king had sons by another.' Charming.

There is a surviving image of Canute and Emma in *The Book of Life*, made in 1031 and kept in Winchester Cathedral. It was inspired by the passage in the *Book of Revelation* which stated that at Judgement Day the dead would be assessed by what was written about them in a big ledger called the 'Book of Life'. Religious houses kept their own versions containing the names of those guaranteed to go to paradise, and everyone was therefore very keen to be mentioned and avoid being cast into a lake of fire for all eternity. Luckily Emma and Canute got their names in, so they were *definitely* going to heaven. The accompanying picture shows the couple putting an enormous cross on the church's altar, a rare image of an early medieval king, although not much can be said about him except that he has a beard. Canute was described as 'exceptionally tall and strong, and the handsomest of men, all except for his nose, that was thin, high-set and rather hooked'. According to the thirteenth-century Icelandic *Knytlinga Saga*, Cnut had eyes 'better than those of other men, both the handsomer and the keener of their sight'.[6]

The image shows the king beside some cherubic angels, and as he got older Canute became very ostentatious in his religion. He bestowed gifts on the monastery of St Omer in Normandy where he

approached the building crying and beating his breast like a luna-
tic. He also gave a vast cross of gold and silver to the New Minster
at Winchester, burial place of Alfred the Great, as well as others.

However much of this was down to politics. The major power of
the era was the Holy Roman Empire, which basically covered what
is today Germany, although the emperor only had a nominal control over many tiny principalities. He did however, have huge sway
over the pope, and as king of Denmark Canute was aware that if
the empire had the backing of the Vatican it could easily overrun
his kingdom.

The eleventh century is when the 'Dark Ages'[7] really come to
an end and what's called the High Medieval Period starts. It is when
many of the things we think of as medieval, such as stone castles and
cathedrals, are built; it also saw the growth of monasteries and later
the first universities. The role of the pope in European affairs also
became established, and it was only now that he became a powerful
figure in international politics, with huge influence over monarchs.
Partly this was due to the spread of education, which was controlled
by the Church; the Church was also a sort of industry, with monastic orders owning huge chunks of land and heavily involved in things
like animal husbandry (many types of sheep were bred by monks,
and beer especially owes much to them).[8] All of these led to a big
reduction in violence and, in the twelfth century, western Europe's
first renaissance.

As part of his international political strategy Canute had his
daughter Gunnhild married off to the Emperor Henry, although
it went badly wrong. She was accused of adultery and to prove her
innocence had to endure man-to-man combat, which was the way
trials were done, except being a woman she could nominate someone instead to fight her accuser. Unfortunately this accuser was a
giant and no one would take him on except a page boy who won
against all odds. Gunnhild was cleared of the allegation and refused

to ever sleep with her husband again. (In retrospect divorce lawyers are not the absolute worst things in the world.)

A paranoid man by nature—perhaps reasonably—Canute eventually fell out with most of his cronies, including Thorkell, who he had arrested in 1021. Two years later there was a reconciliation, mainly because Thorkell had a big army of super-vikings with him. As a result, Thorkell ruled Denmark in Canute's name, and they swapped children as hostages, with Thorkell's son ending up marrying Canute's niece (another Gunnhild). Hardicnut, Canute's son by Emma, lived with Thorkell in Denmark, leaving his mother and father at the age of five to be raised by a man who his father had tried to kill; unsurprisingly he didn't grow up to be the most mentally balanced of young men.

Having already conquered England, in 1025 Canute invaded Norway with a Danish-English army, but on this occasion Olaf the Stout, now King Olaf II, beat him. After the battle Canute and his brother-in-law Ulf spent an evening playing chess. Canute made a mistake, Ulf took one of his knights and an argument broke out. The following morning Canute got one of his underlings to kill Ulf—in church.

In 1028 Canute finally conquered Norway and some of Sweden, and went to Rome for a coronation.[9] He liked the idea of being a Christian monarch but in reality he was a Viking, and still came from that world. By his law 'the heirs of a thegn who stood nearest to the king were required to give him two saddled and two unsaddled horses; two swords; four spears and shields; a helmet, corselet, and fifty mancuses of gold, before they took to their inheritance.'

Canute died in 1035, aged just forty; had he lived longer he might have established a lasting union between England and Scandinavia. As it is, despite being reasonably popular at the time, he is now mostly just remembered as the man with a slightly rude name who shouted at the sea.

Geoffrey of Cambrai wrote an epigram about Canute saying of him that: 'Often leaving the joyous banquets of his own table, He became a companion of poor monks. Putting aside pomp, amid a needy crowd, a fellow slave, he served the slaves of God'. Well, that's one way of looking at it.

CHAPTER FIVE

Lady Godiva

According to Emma's book, her son with Canute was named Hardicnut, 'tough knot', because it was prophesized that he would excel over 'all men of his time by superiority in all high qualities'. Alas no. As with King Edgar, a great king was succeeded by two sons from two different wives, neither of whom were up to much. After the old Viking's death in 1035 and his no doubt instantaneous ascension to Heaven the leading earls met by the Thames to decide who got to succeed him; the river was the barrier between Wessex and Mercia and the senior men of the two old kingdoms were divided over the not-very-thrilling choice.

At first Elfgifu's son Harold, nicknamed Harefoot because of his swiftness of action, was proclaimed regent, with Hardicnut being nominally in charge of the area south of the Thames, but after two years Harold just made himself full king, as his half brother was stuck in Scandinavia.

Harold was unpopular, described as 'an arrogant fellow of bad character',[1] and Queen Emma put a rumor around that he was actually the son of a priest and a servant girl, a common myth down the ages put about by enemies of the ruling monarch.[2] And over in Normandy Ethelred's sons by Emma, Edward and Alfred, had a far better claim to the throne. Soon a letter was sent to them, supposedly from Emma in England, with the passive-aggressive sign-off 'queen in name only', suggesting they invade and claiming the boys' position was threatened by a usurper who was gaining supporters, i.e. Harold. Emma later claimed in her biography that the letter was a forgery, organized by Harefoot, although she may have been embarrassed that she had encouraged such a cack-handed invasion by her sons that was inevitably going to end badly. This was the first Norman invasion of England, and it wasn't quite as successful as the later one.

The two young princes arrived in the country separately, although we can't know what they planned to do afterwards and who got to be king. Edward got close to Southampton but seeing that the coast was well defended, sensibly headed back to spend another few years sponging off relatives in France. His brother Alfred went via Flanders and then to Kent, where he was met by Canute's former sidekick Earl Godwin, now one of the richest men in the country.

Godwin, a thegn from Sussex, had risen to become effective ruler of the country under Canute while the old Viking was either in Scandinavia or crying in front of a church. He was the son of Wulfnoth, the nobleman who had a sea battle with Eadric, and there was something a bit shady about his origins. Godwin may have been of noble family, one theory being that his father descended from Alfred the Great's brother Ethelred, and people rarely rose from nothing at the time. Another story is that during the 1016 invasion Canute's then friend Ulf was lost and helped by a handsome youth herding cattle, and this young man, Godwin, ended up marrying Ulf's sister. Alternatively Godwin's first wife may have been Canute's sister, who was basically a human trafficker exporting English girls to Denmark, until she was killed by a bolt of lightning, which one or two people thought fair.[3] By 1020 Godwin was Earl of Wessex, and also accompanied Canute on various military expeditions, eventually becoming *bajulus*, or bailiff of the kingdom; with his second wife Gytha, a Danish aristocrat, he had six sons and four daughters.

Canute was impressed with Godwin's 'intelligence, his stead-fastness, his strength and courage, and his eloquence',[4] and he was widely praised: 'Rather than acting proudly, he became a father figure to all good men. Gentle by nature and education, he treated inferiors and equals alike with courtesy,' according to one historian, although his treatment of Prince Alfred was less commendable.

Godwin took Alfred and his men to Guildford, just south of London, but overnight his forces disappeared and at first dawn the Frenchmen found themselves surrounded by Harold's soldiers, who killed most of them and took Alfred away.

Godwin may have been in on the plot, or he may have just been ordered by the king to hand Alfred over (Norman chroniclers blame him, but they blame the Godwins for everything, and Emma did not seem to hold him responsible) Alfred was taken to East Anglia where his eyes were gouged out, and he died soon after; strangely Emma's biography, when recording this tragedy, features two comedy eyes beside the text, a sort of primitive emoji that seems in poor taste.

Suffice it to say this didn't do much for Harold's already low levels of popularity; but while the king was widely hated, no one hated him more than his half brother Hardicnut, who had been in Denmark the whole time getting angrier and angrier about not being king of England. Hardicnut had his own problems, largely having to do with King Magnus of Norway, Olaf the Stout's son who had become king in 1035 after Harefoot's mother Elfgifu and brother Sweyn had been forced out.[5] However in 1039 Magnus and Hardicnut made a treaty, agreeing that if one of them died first without an heir the other should inherit all their kingdoms; this would prove to be a critical moment in English history after Magnus's insane uncle turned up.

The following year Hardicnut was about to invade from Denmark, and had arrived in Bruges where he learned that Harold had died of 'elfshot', that is attacked by elves, the diagnosis for viruses people couldn't understand at the time. Hardicnut then had Harold's body decapitated and thrown in a bog, before drinking himself to death at a wedding reception.

They weren't a very sophisticated royal family.

Emma's son by Canute was not much better than his predecessor, and by all accounts as roundly hated, but he did have a strange childhood, and had not seen his mother since the age of five. Hardicnut took the chance to punish various people he blamed for Alfred's death, among them Godwin, who appeased the king by giving him a warship which could carry eighty men and then got various magnates from across the country to swear oaths on his behalf.

The new king soon made himself immensely unpopular by quadrupling taxes, and responded to a tax revolt in Worcester by flattening the town in 1041 after two officials were murdered. This policy, where royal officials rode into town and simply killed lots of people and burned down loads of houses, seems a bit excessive to modern eyes and, while it was standard practise, it didn't tend to win him fans.

In nearby Coventry, Leofric, Earl of Mercia, was given the task of enforcing the new and unpopular tax, much to the dismay of his people, as well as his compassionate blonde wife Godgifu, 'God's gift'. In perhaps one of those moments when men promise their other half something without really paying attention to the conversation, Leofric pledged to Godgifu that he'd abolish the tax if she would 'Ride naked before all the people, through the market of the town.' Godgifu, or Godiva as she was later called, did just this, with her hair covering her modesty and accompanied by two horsemen.[6] The story about the locals agreeing to look away, however, is a later addition, as is the bit about one village idiot, Thomas, suffering blindness as punishment for looking at her, from which we get the phrase 'Peeping Tom' (the link between looking at naked women and blindness is a myth common to many cultures, not to mention schoolyards).

It became the most memorable tax protest in history. Only a couple of hundred people lived in Coventry at the time, but as it grew the Lady Godiva pageant became its main attraction, and thousands were turning up by the seventeenth century.[7]

Hardicnut ruled for only two years, his awful reign unexpectedly ending at the wedding of one of his cronies, Canute's standard bearer Tofi the Proud, who was marrying Gytha, daughter of one Osgod Clapa. The party was held in Lambeth, on the south bank of the Thames, and in line with Viking tradition huge amounts of alcohol had been consumed; such drinking parties could go on for eight days, and it was considered hugely impolite to refuse a drink when offered one of their near-lethal concoctions. The king had been boozing and was in the middle of the speech when he collapsed, ending Canute's dynasty in rather ignominious style.

The kindest thing that could be remarked of Hardicnut came from Henry of Huntingdon, who said his court was 'laid four times a day with royal sumptuousness', that is, he could organize a good drinking session.

The last of Canute's line was buried at the Old Minster in Winchester and Emma paid for a very costly relic to be laid there, supposedly the head of St Valentine, who at the time was just known as a Roman priest who had been murdered, and had yet to become associated with courting couples and the multibillion dollar card and flowers industry. Whether it was actually St Valentine's head, or just the head of some random man, God alone knows.

CHAPTER SIX

Edward, Patron Saint of Divorcees

It was unfortunate for Ethelred that, out of sixteen children, only one son survived until middle age, and he was a bit of a drip. Edward 'the Confessor' had had to flee England when he was just thirteen and grew up in Normandy with his uncle, Duke Richard. Although he was more of a Norman than an Englishman, he had an even worse relationship with his mother than Ethelred did, which is saying something.

St Edward—'confessor' means 'pious' rather than guilty, and just referred to someone who was holy enough to be a martyr but hadn't actually been martyred—became a cult figure in later years, and by the low standards of his predecessors he was certainly gentle. However, he ended up with a halo mainly because of the back-stabbing politics of the era, a timely biography commissioned by his wife, and by later Norman attempts to smear his archenemy, Earl Godwin; although building Westminster Abbey obviously helped.

Edward was largely considered pious because he didn't talk during church services, as most people did, but just sat there staring into space, as people do now. He also initiated the tradition where the king would heal the victims of a skin disease called scrofula just by touching them, and this practise of the king's evil, where the monarch touched the sick once a year, continued until the eighteenth century.[1] The illness in question, a form of tuberculosis, often went into remission on its own and was never fatal, so people naturally attributed it to the monarch's hand.

Edward was not exactly saintly—more weird than anything. In the words of one historian, 'the personality described by eye-witnesses is that of a . . . neurotic with a tendency to paranoia and possessed of a fearsome temper that often made him impervious to reason'.[2] While 'his "saintly" detachment can be read in quite another way, as the "schizoid" alienation of the classic lone wolf, who has decided that since no one cares for him he in turn will care for nobody'. Edward also had 'an elephantine memory for slights and an ability to bear grudges eternally'.

Freud would probably have blamed his mother, with whom he played a starring role in a horrific family psychodrama. As a child she abandoned him to go and live with her Scandinavian lover, who had driven Edward's father to an early grave, and after Canute's death she ignored her son and then actively conspired against him. She doesn't appear to have liked Edward (he also hardly got a mention in her book) and he seems to have actively hated her.

Edward had been invited over to England by Hardicnut, and after his untimely ending found himself king, the royal line of Alfred restored once again. However he could not free himself from his mother's control, as she was not only the richest woman in England, but also controlled the treasury. And so on taking charge Edward conspired with the leading magnates Godwin and Leofric, and had his mother arrested and put on trial, one of the suggested reasons being her alleged affair with Stigand, a slightly dubious bishop who would later be excommunicated by five different popes. Emma was tried not by twelve men good and true, which didn't come about for another two centuries, but by walking over nine red hot ploughshares, the sharp part of a plough, trial by ordeal believed to be the most effective way of determining whether someone was guilty. Courtroom drama ensued, however, when she survived this test, and Edward, satisfied by her innocence, restored her lands. Emma was so brave during her trial that after doing the walk she asked when it began, only to be told it was over; the story comes from Emma's own book and is probably not entirely true, or at least it got lots of basic facts wrong, such as mentioning a bishop who didn't arrive in the country until later.

Afterwards Emma turned to Magnus of Norway and tried to get him to overthrow her own son. Magnus had his problems at home but had written a letter to Edward claiming he was rightful king because Hardicnut had promised him the throne, but stating that he couldn't be bothered doing anything about it right now. In the autumn of 1047 for a few weeks it looked like the Norwegians would invade, but on October 25 Magnus died.

Maybe because of his overbearing mother, the Confessor grew into a gentle, slightly weak man; he was so pale as to be almost albino, obsessed with religion, and interested only in praying rather than the two main pursuits of kingship—fighting and fornicating. As a man of God, Edward's grand ambition was to build an abbey to rival St Paul's in London, a 'West minster'. Whether his religious devotion was worth it in the end is doubtful, as the new abbey cost 10 percent of the kingdom's income, when in retrospect building a few castles or training some archers would have been a better idea.

Later, though, this rather weedy, mysterious, pale, sex-scared man—the sort who probably would get harassed by louts today if he lived in rundown government housing—was edged out as patron saint of England by the more manly St George, despite the latter being a) foreign and b) nonexistent. As it is, Edward is the patron saint of divorcees and difficult marriages, and is certainly a good choice for that position, having married into a family of half-Viking nouveau riche gangsters.

Edward's reign was dominated by conflict with Earl Godwin, now the biggest landowner and powerbroker in the land. Although Harold Godwinson would die heroically as England's last native king, his family were mostly a bunch of yobs who were involved in several murders, and who had risen to power through sheer violence and intimidation.

Edward also blamed Godwin for his brother's death, so when the king came to be crowned the earl, with gangland-style largesse, gave him a warship even larger than the one he gave Hardicnut, big enough to fit 120 men, decorated with 'a golden lion' and a winged and golden dragon that 'affrights the sea, and belches fire with triple tongue', lined with tasteful 'patrician purple.'

The Godwin family increased their power by appointing allies to key Church positions, some of whom didn't appear to be very religious. The worst offender was Stigand, who enjoyed an annual income of £3,000 and was widely seen as corrupt, and excommunicated by Rome for holding two sees at the same time in order to rake in the revenues; by the time of the Norman invasion he was, after the king and the Godwin family, the richest man in England.

In contrast to the gentle, sexless king, Godwin's six sons were never likely to be candidates for sainthood. The eldest, Sweyn, was the most psychotic: in a notorious incident he kidnapped Eadgifu, the abbess of Leominster, on the way back from invading Wales, and 'kept her as long as it suited him, and then let her go home'. Whether it was consensual or rape it was considered appalling to carry on in that way with a bride of Christ, and to make it worse they were related.[3] Afterwards he took refuge with his Danish cousin Bjorn, volunteering to fight for Denmark in yet another war against Norway (although he seemed to have spent much time fighting with Danes) and eventually persuaded Bjorn to raid the Isle of Wight with him— and then murdered him. Even by the low standards of the period this was considered shocking and Sweyn Godwinson was declared *nithing*, 'nothing', without any social standing and therefore legitimate for anyone to kill—although eventually he was allowed back.[4]

Second son Harold was far more sensible. Immensely brave, tall at 5'11" (5'8" was the male average), exceptionally good-looking and fond of women, he was a feared leader but also much loved by his men for his affability and good humor. He was also incredibly strong, and by all accounts, even hostile Norman ones, he was an extremely charismatic leader.

Tostig, brother number three, was linked to a string of murders. While as a young man he was popular—even Edward liked him—and a devoted husband, Tostig later appears to have gone totally insane. The three younger brothers we hear less of, especially the youngest Wulfnoth, who appears to have spent his entire adult life in a dungeon.

King Edward hated Godwin, but perhaps having no choice but to recognize his power, married the earl's daughter Edith. Had Edward and Edith had children, our history would have been very different, and while there has been speculation that the king may have been gay—one historian wrote that 'it should be noticed that he was, rightly or wrongly, credited with no bastards, something rather unusual at the time'[5] or asexual, his hatred for his father-in-law probably can't have helped. Whatever a man's sexual preferences, being married to a woman whose father helped murder your brother is going to make things awkward. Edward the Confessor and his wife seemed to have been reasonably happy, although he spoke of her as his 'beloved daughter', which doesn't suggest a marriage burning with passion, and she used to lie by his feet to show her humility. Much of this comes from Edith's own biography, which was written in 1066 just as the country was falling apart, and painted her in particular as the model wife; the *In Vita Edith* describes her as 'an incomparable bride, virtuous, intelligent, well-educated, talented and generous'. But then she also compared her father Godwin to

Jesus, in that terrible accusations were made against both of them but essentially they were both really good guys.

The king's relations with the Godwins reached crisis point in October 1050 when the archbishop of Canterbury died, followed in January 1051 by the archbishop of York. These were the two most important Church positions and Edward put Norman cronies of his into the roles, which could only have been seen as an insult to Godwin. Worse still, the new primate Robert of Jumieges was outspoken against the Earl of Wessex, publically saying he intended to do to Edward what he had done to Alfred; not the most diplomatic of language. Even Edward was embarrassed by this and did not attend Jumieges's investiture as archbishop because he was such a liability.

Robert was one of many Normans and other Frenchmen who had come over with Edward in 1042 as his escort and so the Godwins were able to present themselves as the anti-French party, which always works in English politics. Among the Normans already in England was Edward's sister's son Earl Ralph the Timid, who had inherited the earldom of Hereford and earned his nickname after running away from the Welsh in 1055. He died in 1057 and had he survived England may well have had a King Ralph in 1066;[6] another Norman, Regenbald, was made royal chancellor in 1062, and the foreigners being given good grants of land and cushy jobs possibly didn't help the king's popularity.[7]

The following year Eustace of Boulogne, the husband of Edward's sister and a major ally, made a diplomatic visit to England. It got off to a shaky start when Eustace stabbed to death an innkeeper in Dover when the man refused to let him stay the night, then started a brawl that left twenty of the townspeople dead along with nineteen of Eustace's men; not the most successful of diplomatic visits then.

Afterwards Edward called a council at Gloucester in which Robert of Jumieges accused Godwin of conspiring against him.[8]

In response the king ordered that Dover be harried, but Godwin refused. Harrying was quite a typical response to a crime committed in a town; as well as Hardicnut in Worcester King Eadred had harried Thetford, and his successor Edgar had done the same to Thanet, but Godwin, quite reasonably, demanded that the other side of the story be heard. And so Edward exiled the entire family, half of the Godwin clan going to Ireland and the others to the continent. Edward sent his wife to live in a convent as punishment, and she was 'despoiled of all her lands and movables'.

From 1051, when the country was now in chaos, the coins in England began to be issued with PACX on one side, 'Peace'—which rather suggests that all wasn't entirely well.

But Edward could not rule without the Godwin family, who were vastly rich, in fact probably richer than the king. Crucially the Earls Leofric and Siward, the largest landowners in the midlands and north respectively, refused to fight against Godwin, so the following year he returned, arriving on the Isle of Wight, and Edward's Norman friends left the county. Robert of Jumieges fled from London to Essex where he 'lighted on a crazy ship', as a chronicler enigmatically called it; with the Godwins restored, Stigand was made archbishop despite Robert of Jumieges already being alive, and Stigand still being bishop of Winchester. Crucially, however, Robert of Jumieges may have taken Godwin's youngest son Wulfnoth with him to Normandy as hostage.

But just as the Godwins were winning, eldest son Sweyn, in a final twist, decided he was going to go on pilgrimage to Jerusalem to seek penance for all the terrible things he had done. The trip to the Holy Land was an extremely hazardous one, not just because of pirates and robbers, but also the various diseases that westerners caught there; and Sweyn died on the way back, of a cold of all things.

Meanwhile Edward's mother had finally passed away,[9] and to mark the occasion he had a new portrait done of himself on coins.

Instead of 'a debased classical image, appeared the head and shoulders of a bearded warrior wearing a conical helmet and holding a sceptre before his face . . . it was an unusually virile design'.[10] It seemed to be some sort of midlife crisis for the king.

The feud ended in 1053 when Godwin gave himself a stroke while sitting on a bar stool at Edward's palace; by one obviously biased account later put about by supporters of William the Conqueror, the old man choked on a piece of bread as he explained to the king: 'If that is true [that I killed your brother] then may God let this piece of bread choke me. [Choke].'

But the Godwin clan continued to grow in strength. In 1054, Edward's military commander Siward of Northumbria invaded Scotland and overthrew the king who, were it not for a sixteenth-century playwright, would have remained an obscure character locked in the history departments of university libraries. The real Macbeth was nothing like the tortured Shakespearean murderer and won the crown reasonably fairly, if violently, after Duncan 'the Diseased' invaded his fiefdom. Although the English won, Siward's son Osbeorn and his nephew, another Siward, were killed and in 1055 Siward died, leaving a surviving son Waltheof who was only a boy. This presented a new opportunity for the Godwins and so Tostig was made Earl of Northumbria, which turned out to be a not-very-wise decision.

After his father's death Harold became the 'under king' who effectively ruled the country, led armies and even undertook trips to the continent; by now Edward had basically given up on life anyway. However in 1056, while Harold was on the continent, there was trouble in Wales and unfortunately the English response was led by Leofgar, bishop of Hereford, who as can be guessed by his job title wasn't a skilled military tactician. Leofgar had been Harold's clerk and supporter, and even wore his hair long and with a moustache, the Godwin fashion and seen as very racy and not appropriate for a churchman. The bishop decided to lead a group of priests in battle against the Welsh leader Gruffydd and they all got killed at Glasbury-on-Wye—a lesson in why bishops shouldn't really lead armies. The militia of England was called, and an 'unwieldy force, wholly unfitted to mountain warfare' led an expedition that a contemporary remembered fondly by 'the misery and the marching and the hosting and the toil and the loss of men and horses'.

The Anglo-Saxons and Britons, as the Welsh were still called, had been almost at continuous war since the former had arrived from Germany; in the eighth century Offa of Mercia resolved the issue by building a great dyke to keep the Welsh out, which now survives as a walking route, but from time to time there were raids. What especially annoyed the Saxons was the Welsh bardic tradition, which 'surrounded their mayhem and rapine with an aura of legend, so that cattle-thieves, rapists and murderers were presented in Welsh bardic tradition as mythical heroes'.[11] This has been a continuing theme of Celtic resistance down the centuries, where often the most charismatic and effective leaders were also bandits and murderers; the modern equivalent might be the glorified accounts of romantic figures like Che Guevara that conveniently don't mention all the murders they carried out.

In 1063 there was another uprising in Wales, and Harold and Tostig led an army west. The conflict had began in what is now Newport because English merchants refused to pay a fee to the Welsh, and so Harold's assembled army ravaged the area and violated the Welsh church of St Gwynllyw, but stopped when some cheese started to bleed and they got scared.

Harold's invasion of Wales left 'not one that pisseth against a wall', a chronicler said; he was also the first to instigate those laws stating that any Welshman found on this side of Offa's Dyke with a weapon should have his right hand cut off, some of which are still technically the law in England.[12] It was the Welsh tradition to behead their enemies but Harold made such an impression on them that the Welsh chose to decapitate their own leader, Gruffydd, and send it to him rather than face the consequences; Harold gave it to King Edward as a gift.

Although the Confessor had vaguely promised the crown to a number of people there was an obvious choice of successor. One of Edmund Ironside's young sons, another Edward, had survived childhood in faraway Hungary, and so in 1055 King Edward sent Bishop Ealdred of Worcester to Germany to ask the emperor's permission for Edward 'the Exile' to come to England. The bishop spent an entire year at the court in Cologne waiting for an answer from the emperor; finally however in 1057 civil war in Hungary meant the Exile was willing to return. Edward, who had grown up in Hungary and had a Hungarian wife and three Hungarian-born children, had returned out of a sense of duty and wasn't particularly keen on the idea.

However after travelling all the way back to England, he died a week after arriving, having not even met the king yet. The death was naturally suspicious, and while the Godwins could have been behind it, he might also have been poisoned by Normans, too, since that was more their style. Edward had left a son, Edgar, but he was just a child of five.

Things were made more complicated because of Harold's brother Tostig, who had become wildly unpopular as Earl of Northumbria, largely on account of his over-enthusiastic law and order policy. Northumbria was an alien place to most southerners, there were few passable roads between north and south, and the region was also far more heavily Danish, especially around York, which retained large elements of Norse dialect until fairly recently.[13]

Edward had never once been up north in his entire reign—in fact like many upper-class southern English people he knew France much better than anything beyond the Trent—and Harold barely went north if he could avoid it. The region was dangerous, so unsafe this it could not be traversed except in a large group, and the earl, already unpopular for being a southerner, had apparently been too enthusiastic in trying to restore law and order. The *Anglo-Saxon Chronicle* said of Tostig: 'Not a few charged that glorious earl with being too cruel; and he was accused of punishing disturbers more for the desire of their confiscated property than for love of justice.' One of the *Chronicles* also said that Tostig was 'occasionally a little too enthusiastic in attacking evil', which sounds like a delicate way of describing an absolute psychopath.

From late 1064 a number of Northumbrian aristocrats were murdered, which everyone attributed to Tostig; over Christmas 1064 Gamel, son of Orm, and Ulf, son of Dolin, the two leading northern leaders, were killed. On December 28 another earl, Gospatric, was slain. It was also rumoured that Tostig had earlier tried to have Gospatric murdered on pilgrimage to Rome when they were attacked by bandits.

Although the Normans exaggerated Tostig's crimes, there was certainly an air of general seediness about the English court of this time. William of Malmesbury, who was half-Norman and half-English, made a list of all the sins the aristocracy committed, which had brought divine disaster in the form of invasion. Among these, he said, they 'Give up to luxury and wantonness' and 'they did not go to church in the morning as Christians should, but merely, in a careless manner, heard matins and masses from a hurrying priest in their chambers, among the blandishments of their wives.' On top of this 'they used to eat till they were surfeited and drink till they were sick' and 'one of their customs, repugnant to nature, was to sell their female servants, when pregnant by them and after they had satisfied their lust, either to public prostitution or slavery. They wore gold bracelets, and short garments down to the knee, shaved their beards and had their skin tattooed.' Well, they weren't a genteel crowd, certainly.

In October that year discontent with Tostig, probably provoked by a tax, finally led to an uprising in the north, led by two brothers from the old ruling house of Northumbria, Edwin and Morcar, who were barely even teenagers. The two were the grandsons of Leofric and Godgifu (of naked horse-riding fame), and after the death of their father Elfgar felt they were deprived of status. The revolt began with the murder of Tostig's men in York, and spread south as far as the Thames, threatening the country with yet another war.

Harold acted as mediator, and probably agreed to exile Tostig and make the two brothers Earls of Northumbria and Mercia, while marrying their sister (even though he had a long-term handfast, Edith Swan-Neck, with whom he had a number of children). His new wife, another Edith, happened to be the widow of Gruffydd, whose head was last seen carried out around by Harold—small world!

Presumably the quid pro quo was that they would support his claim to the throne, and so Harold discarded his mistress and brother, who now accused him of engineering the whole thing. Some accounts suggest that Harold and Tostig were rivals from early on, and a later story has the young brothers fighting at the royal court as youngsters.[14] The embittered Tostig fled with his wife to Flanders.

By now Edward was dying, and the country was filled with foreboding. The year 1065 began with a sense of impending doom, for it was considered bad luck when the Feast of the Annunciation coincided with Good Friday. As the ditty went: 'When Our Lord falls on Our Lady's lap, England shall have a dire mishap'. (It sounds like the sort of thing where they came up with the ditty first and the superstition later.) Now the final days of that year were marked by terrible storms. The noblemen of England came from all around the country to feast together at Thorney Island, where Edward's grand abbey dedicated to St Peter was being built. Although the church was not ready, it was consecrated anyway on December 28 because Edward was not long for this world, although he was still too sick to attend.

Edward had been dying for some time, all the while mumbling and babbling in his sleep, when everyone just wanted him to name a successor. The king retired to bed where he saw an apocalyptic vision, in which England was consumed with fire and abandoned to the devil, all because of its peoples' wickedness, especially of its churchmen. Edward in his delirium said the leading bishops of the country 'were not the servants of God; they were in league with the devil.' Archbishop Stigand, irritated at this babble, suggested that the 'king was broken with disease and knew not what he said'.

In Edward's derangement he said two monks warned him that England was cursed by God and would suffer evil spirits for a year and a day. No prayers would prevent this, the monks told him, and the curse would only be lifted if a tree was felled halfway down its trunk, and then came together by itself and bore fresh fruit: 'Only then would the sins of the people be forgiven and England find respite from its suffering.' Not the sort of straight answer you want in a time of national crisis.

As expected, no tree put itself together and there followed twelve months that would be remembered as the year of three kings, the year when the Anglo-Saxon world was destroyed and England changed forever, a date so familiar that people are advised to not use it as their PIN number. Edward's great church became known as the West Minster, giving its name to the area which is now Britain's government; despite the effort and cost involved, Westminster Abbey was knocked down in the thirteenth century anyway and rebuilt.

Edward had told Harold: 'I commend [Edith] and all the kingdom to your protection.' It was in effect a nomination and after the Confessor died on January 5 the Witan chose Harold as king; he was crowned on the same day as Edward's funeral.

Godfrey of Cambrai also wrote an epigram for King Edward, stating: 'He confronted his enemies not with war but with peace. And no one thought to violate his peace.' Which wasn't quite true.

CHAPTER SEVEN

'A Savage, Barbarous and Horrible Race of Inhuman Disposition'

Duke William of Normandy was out hunting when the news was gently broken to him that Harold was king. The duke had long maintained that his cousin Edward had promised him the throne, and that Harold had sworn to support him; now, whether or not he believed his own rather tenuous argument, the duke would embark on an invasion of epic proportions.

The Normans were not the sort of enemies anyone would wish for. Although exposed to classical Latin culture and Christianity, these French speakers were even more aggressive than their Norse ancestors, and the cultural influences of the civilized south only clothed their barbaric tendencies like a nightclub doorman wearing an ill-fitting dinner jacket.

However it did make them more sophisticated in their violence, to which their entire way of life was geared: they cut their hair short in the more military Roman style, they bred a special battle-ready war horse from Arab stallions, and developed archery in a way that would be decisive in 1066. Even their favourite (and only) cerebral activity, chess, brought back from Arabia and subsequently introduced into England, reflected their main interest—conquest.[1] Originally from Persia—check comes from the Farsi for king, *shah*— it was not the effete game it is today, and matches would regularly end in fights with the pieces, heavy and up to four inches tall, being used to solve disputes. One later medieval English king almost killed an opponent after throwing a chess piece at him.

Even before their conquest of England, the Normans had gathered a reputation for violence, turning up all over Europe for fights that they seemed to hugely enjoy. Hervey de Glanville, who led an attack on Lisbon, asked of them: 'Who does not know that the Norman race refuses no effort in the continual exercise of its power? Its warlikeness is ever hardened by adversity, it is not easily upset by difficulties nor, when difficulties have been overcome, does it allow itself to be conquered by slothful inactivity, for it has learned always to shake off the vice of sloth with activity.'[2]

Others were not so keen on the 'ferocious Normans', as William of Apulia called them. One Lombard prince, facing Norman warlords in southern Italy, described 'a savage, barbarous and horrible race of inhuman disposition'.[3] Another Italian called them a 'cunning and vengeful people'. Even Henry of Huntingdon, half-Norman himself, said they 'surpassed all other people in their unparalleled savagery'.

The militaristic nature of Norman society was a product of geography; in a highly disputed part of western Europe where various tribes fought for control, only the most aggressive tended to survive (a similar thing happened much later with the goose-stepping army-state Prussia uniting Germany).

Norman society, like all of northern France, was also directed by a new concept: chivalry. From the French word for knight or horseman, chivalry had probably started in Germany in the tenth century, and later it became 'an international brotherhood with peculiar religious rites and esoteric morality'. But at this point it was essentially a cult of violence which encouraged young men to look down on reading and writing as something that only priests did; instead men of noble breeding learned to train from a young age in order to do one thing in life—fight. As with many male subcul-. tures, it saw education as being effeminate, while trade was viewed as low-status and beneath them.

Obviously this worldview would end up having a destructive influence and cause countless deaths, but the warlikeness of the northern French helped them to expand across the West, so that by 1350 twelve of Catholic Europe's fifteen monarchs were Frankish in origin. [4] During this period the entire region became Frankified, which is why you probably know someone called William, Charles, Henry, Robert or Richard but not many Eadrics or Hardicnuts, and also why Europeans today are known generically in various Asian languages as 'firang' (in the Vietnam War this is what the locals called the Americans).

And the Franks were not only the prime movers in the Crusades but in places like Spain and today's Poland they led military cam- paigns against Muslims and pagans, and were ruthless colonists in Ireland and elsewhere. The Normans were very much part of this scene, and some historians say the takeover of 1066 would be better described as the 'Frankish Conquest'.

Driving this expansion was the cult of the knight, so that as one historian put it, 'Chivalry in later ages may have had merits, but in the eleventh century it was a social disaster. It produced a super- fluity of conceited illiterate young men who had no ideals except to rise and hunt and fight, whose only interest in life was violence and the glory they saw in it . . . they were no good at anything else, and despised any peaceful occupation'.[5] These young men 'just by exist- ing . . . created wars'. On top of this there was the Norman system of primogenitor, which gave all the inheritance to the eldest son, and this drove the relentless Norman expansion, first to England and later Wales and Ireland, led by landless aristocratic younger brothers.

Normandy was not only externally aggressive to its neighbours, but internally very violent too. Private war was so common that the Church managed to get everyone to agree to a compromise where war was banned between Wednesday evening and Monday morning, the so-called 'Truce of God' that was the best they could manage.

Norman boys would start their careers as pages, then become squires, and eventually knights in their early twenties. It was a violent life and lots of young Normans died during their apprenticeships; one lord named Giroie lost both his sons to violent horseplay, one struck by a lance and another with a rock while wrestling, but Normans seemed to consider this a reasonable price to pay.

Even before conquering England, the Normans had rather improbably ended up ruling southern Italy, which all started when some of them began using it as a stopping off point on the way back from pilgrimages in the Holy Land. The first Norman principality was established at Aversa in Campania, close to Naples; it began when in AD 999 a group of forty Normans arrived in Salerno, on the way back from Palestine, and found the town under siege from a Saracen army. The locals asked them to help and this tiny force ended up beating a much larger Muslim force; the holidaymakers went off to Normandy but promised locals they'd be back, and by 1015 they were. Then a Lombard aristocrat asked them to conquer Apulia from the Byzantine Greeks, and although the Greeks beat them in 1018 they stuck around and eventually took charge, led by the twelve sons of an especially virile Norman called Tancred. Their first leader, Tancred's son William Ironarm, became count in 1042, followed by his brother Drogo.

The Normans had become so powerful that in 1052 Pope Leo IX set up a coalition to get rid of them, a force comprising Greeks, Italians and Germans that attacked in June 1053. However the Normans, despite being in a constant state of internecine feuding at the time, managed to unite and beat the invaders, led by another of Tancred's sons, Robert Guiscard, literally 'the Weasel', so called because of his cunning. He had arrived in Italy with just five horsemen and thirty foot soldiers but ended up running half the country.

The Normans then captured Leo IX and pledged their loyalty to him even as they kept him prisoner until he changed his mind about them. Now almost in charge of all of southern Italy, the Normans invaded Sicily in 1061, and succeeded. At that time the island had long been ruled by various Muslim leaders, although it was now split between three rival Arab states all in a state of mutual hostility. The Normans ruled Sicily for another century and a half until conquered by the even more violent and uncouth Angevins, from the region of Anjou just to the south of Normandy. Sicily is the one place where the Normans are remembered rather fondly, partly because they drove out the Arabs but also because, compared to the Angevins they were like twenty-first-century Scandinavian progressives.

William the Bastard

William the Conqueror came from a long line of tough men, but Norman leaders had to be, faced with almost constant conflict with their neighbors in Flanders, Brittany and Maine, as well as the king of France, who was in theory their overlord. They also had unrest at home; William's grandfather Richard II had dealt with a peasants' uprising by cutting off all their hands and feet. However the biggest challenge was the rivalry between aristocrats so that no Norman duke was ever safe from his relatives, who were generally as venal and violent as he was.

William 'the bastard' had it worse than most. His father Robert had supposedly first fallen for William's mother Herleve when he spied her bare legs as she washed by a river in her hometown of Falaise, a story that the medievals found endearing rather than quite sinister and creepy.[6] Herleve is supposed to have been the daughter of a tanner or undertaker,[7] and William's enemies said his mother stank of the tannery—but people who made this joke tended to have body parts chopped off, which proved remarkably effective as a form of censorship. Also, the story about Robert spying her most likely came from the people who worked at Falaise Castle, who used to charge people to see where it all happened, even though the window from which Robert supposedly spotted her wasn't built until the twelfth century.

Medieval chroniclers certainly seemed to have been sordidly fascinated by this romantic tryst; the Norman chronicler Wace described how Herleve came to Robert's room and they remained awake for some time and 'for I do not wish to say anything more about the way a man disports himself with his beloved'. After this Herleve is supposed to have fallen asleep and had a dream in which her 'inward parts' began to grow into an enormous tree, so big that eventually the whole of Normandy and England was under its shadow.

William's father Robert 'the Magnificent' afterwards succeeded his elder brother Richard as duke, after he died in mysterious circumstances. It's often thought Robert poisoned him, since the Normans were always poisoning people, and Robert clearly had the most to gain from his brother's death and had previously risen in revolt against him. However it's also worth noting that in the medieval period deaths from accidental food poisoning were also absurdly common since people didn't practise basic kitchen hygiene. Robert the Magnificent was also known as 'Robert the Liberal' although this was due to his generous donations to friendly churchmen, rather than any LGBT activism. Another nickname, the Devil, may have been made up later, but certainly his reign was very violent and dominated by a feud with the Norman aristocracy in which he pillaged church property when it was in the hands of enemies. His own uncle, Archbishop Robert of Rouen, called Duke Robert a 'scourge of God'.

Although illegitimate, William was accepted as Duke Robert's heir, but when his son was only seven the duke decided to go travelling to the Holy Land; historians are puzzled by this decision, which seems insanely irresponsible, especially as he himself knew how ruthless his own relatives were and how vulnerable Normandy was. Robert may have journeyed to the Mediterranean because of the heroic tales from southern Italy, which made him jealous of Robert the Weasel. Another theory is that he felt bad for murdering his brother.

Robert fell sick in Jerusalem and died on his way home, leaving William to grow up in a feud-ridden court where several attempts were made on his life: four guardians were murdered during his childhood. Someone called Odo the Fat killed his first protector, Count Gilbert, and then his tutor Turold. Later Osbern, head of the royal household, was stabbed to death, his throat slashed, by William of Montgomery in William's bedchamber with the young duke in the room. Montgomery was himself later murdered in another feud. After this upbringing William surprisingly grew up to be quite violent and unhinged, and he later said: 'I was schooled in war since childhood'. This wouldn't make him the most reasonable man in later life.

By the time that Edward the Confessor passed away William was nearly forty, and battle-hardened by years of conflict with Normandy's neighbours Maine, Flanders and France. A thick-set and tall man, at five feet eleven, William was exceptionally intelligent but his overriding characteristic was greed. He was 'a cold, grim and overweening ambitious man, who could be extremely harsh and cruel and brooked no opposition',[8] and 'violent but scheming, deadly as a snake', and had a harsh, guttural voice, was very strong and possessed great stamina. All in all he sounds like a terrifying man.

The duke was also virtually teetotal, which stood out in an age when drunkenness was far more common than today. And even more unusually for the time, he was completely faithful to his wife, Matilda of Flanders; in fact it was so expected that aristocratic men would have mistresses that many found William's fidelity a bit creepy and thought he must actually be up to something.

Matilda of Flanders had at first refused to marry a 'bastard', as she put it, and so William rode two hundred fifty miles to Lille, crossing marshland, before arriving at her father's castle, where he threw her to the ground and 'tore her robes with his spurs'. Apparently she was impressed and married him, because she 'recognized that she had met her master' and 'he must be a man of great courage and high daring' to 'come and beat me in my own father's palace'.[9] This sounds unlikely, and it was most likely Norman propaganda to show how manly William was; which says something about how different their attitudes were to ours. With Matilda he had four sons and five or six daughters;[10] strangely she was only four feet two inches tall, a fact confirmed when her grave was later opened.[11]

A rather humorless man, the only things that made William laugh were cruel practical jokes, and he often used violence in jest, which must have been hilarious. On one occasion he beat a forester with an animal bone for questioning his grant to a monastery—this was a joke. Another time, at a meeting held at Easter he gave the grant of property to the Abbey of Holy Trinity in Rouen 'by a knife which the king playfully gave the abbot as if about to stab his hand'. The Normans did not sound like relaxing company to be around.

Both William and Matilda were very devout and each established religious houses. La Trinite, Matilda's abbey, had some of the best relics in northern Europe, among them 'splinters of wood from Christ's manger and Cross, a piece of bread that He had touched, and a strand of His mother Mary's hair', as well as 'the finger of St Cecile, a hair of St Denis, the blood of St George, and even several entire corpses'.[12]

One motivation for this piety was that the couple had been too closely related to marry, and the union was opposed by the pope and the Norman clergy, led by an Italian abbot called Lanfranc. William expelled Lanfranc and his men sacked his abbey; however on his way out of Normandy Lanfranc coincidentally bumped into the duke and the two men spoke and got on. William there and then persuaded him to change his mind (this is how pro-Norman chroniclers put it. We can only imagine what this persuasion consisted of).

Before setting off on his madcap adventure Duke Robert had done the decent thing by Herleve by arranging a marriage for her to a local nobleman, by which she produced two sons, Odo and Robert of Mortaine, and the new duke relied heavily on his mother's relatives throughout his reign, since these were the only people he could trust; he certainly couldn't trust his father's family, many of whom were out to murder him.

Having survived a grim childhood, at nineteen William crushed his first rebellion, at Val-es-Dunes, which was provoked by rival Norman warlords; he charged fearlessly into this first battle, and had fought a series of extremely violent wars since. In one of these rebellions, in 1051, the people of Alençon had taunted William by shouting 'Hides! Hides for the tanner!' a reference to his parentage, which they thought very funny. After William captured the town he paraded thirty-two of its citizens on the bridge and had their hands and feet cut off in view of everyone. It's fair to say William couldn't take a joke.

The year 1053 saw the last internal Norman revolt. A rebel, also called William, was helped by the king of France and it culminated in February 1054 with a brutal battle between Norman and French troops at Mortemer, which the Normans won. After that William became the supreme leader of the region, and King Henry of France, in theory his overlord, never challenged him.

William had beaten all his neighbors, among them rivals Guy of Ponthieu and Eustace of Boulogne; then in 1063 he invaded Maine to the south on some spurious pretext, seizing a castle after paying two children to sneak in and set fire to it. The local count, Walter, was the nephew of Edward the Confessor and so had a very strong claim to be throne of England. He and his wife Bota were taken into Norman custody where predictably soon they died of mysterious causes. William then forcibly married Walter's daughter to his son Robert.

Feudal Anarchy

This period was characterized by what's now called 'feudal anarchy', a situation where real power lay not with kings but with local lords. Because kings had not effectively centralized power yet, and the concept of nations was still vague, if you had a castle and a private army there wasn't much anyone could do to stop you. There was private justice and war against all—generally speaking not the best time to be alive, and much more violent than the later medieval period by which time a local lord couldn't just hang anyone who annoyed him.[13]

The Normans were not more culturally advanced than the Saxons, but in warfare, and in particular cavalry and archery, they were the best. In the eleventh century they had become supreme horse breeders of the 'destrier', which were fourteen hands high, as opposed to the normal ten for a regular horse. Around this period the northern French invented the cavalry charge, which was hugely effective, and terrifying. The Normans also developed kite-shaped shields, which could be used on horseback better that traditional round shields. It was an expensive business: Norman knights would bring four horses to battle, one for riding there, one for battle, one for his squire and another for baggage.

Even Norman priests were known to get involved in fights, including the Conqueror's half brother Bishop Odo who is seen in the Bayeux Tapestry waving a club. Churchmen were only supposed to carry clubs or maces into battle, rather than swords, as they couldn't cut their enemies; although this seems fairly pedantic when the net effect was basically the same.

One advantage the conquerors did not have was their distinctive mail, which we associate as being the classic Norman look, since both sides at Hastings wore these long coats of mail, with a coif around the head. Likewise with the conical helmets with a bar over the nose called a nasel and the neck guard, the 'hauberk', which also became a sign of aristocratic status.[14] In fact the only way to distinguish them was that the Saxons wore moustaches while the northern French were clean shaven, with close-cropped hair.

Chainmail protected against most weapons, although not a direct sword attack or two-handed axe. The battleaxe, the weapon of the English elite *housecarls*, could easily cut through chainmail and the shields of the time; then there was the Viking sword, which was so powerful it was said a man was sliced 'so cleanly in two as he sat in his armour, that the cut only became apparent when, as he rose to shake himself, he fell dead in two halves'.[15] The surprise on his face when he realised!

The Normans had also developed the couched lance, a spear which was between nine and eleven feet and was deadly when thrown (it could also be pulled out of a body easily, and so used again).

Normandy had a population of around a million, roughly half that of England, but because of the violent nature of Norman society William had thirty thousand soldiers at his disposal; Harold had less than half that. England, being largely secure from land invasion, had become less militarized and had not kept up with the most recent innovation, archery, while also falling behind in the breeding of war horses.

William's would be the third Norman invasion of England. After Prince Alfred's poor effort, Duke Robert had attempted one on his cousin Edward's behalf but a wind had scattered his fleet, which landed in the Channel Islands. He then decided that since he was in the area he may as well invade Brittany, which may have been his real intention all along.

Later William would state that Edward promised him the throne and that Harold Godwinson had pledged to support his claim. This is implausible, for even if Edward or Harold had promised the crown to William, which is unlikely, it was not in their power to give it to him anyway, since the Witan chose the monarch.

William claimed that Harold had personally sworn an oath to uphold his title, most likely in 1064, when he visited Normandy. The reason for Harold's journey is a mystery, but it's most likely he went there to bring back his youngest brother Wulfnoth and nephew, Sweyn's son Hakon, both of whom were hostages there for reasons that still remain obscure. Harold may have been lost in a storm while on his way to Flanders, or tricked into crashing, and he and his men were captured by Count Guy of Ponthieu, a notorious hostage taker who was also William's brother-in-law. Ponthieu was infamous for wrecking and went by the custom of '*lagan*', whereby local lord had absolute rights to shipwrecks. It meant people often put out false signals and killed people who were then shipwrecked. Seaside towns often made a living by putting out false lights and then stealing all their goods—wrecking was quite normal until relatively recently.

One of Harold's men was able to alert Duke William that the Earl of Wessex, by far and away the richest man in England and so a great hostage, was being held; William had previously defeated Guy in battle—and killed his brother—and so was able to order him to hand over the Englishmen.

Now a guest/hostage in Normandy, Harold was invited by William to come and fight in a campaign against his neighbor Count Conan of Brittany, and the two appear to have got on well (Harold probably spoke French, as well as a number of languages). Brittany and Normandy were constantly at war, and Conan had some reasons to dislike the people next door as his father Alan III had been poisoned by the Normans. Harold had by all accounts acted very bravely during this battle, and rescued two Norman knights who had got stuck in the quicksand on the border between Brittany and Normandy, a feat of great strength that appears in the Bayeux Tapestry.

Duke William and Earl Harold had got on well despite the obvious awkward issue at hand. William, strangely, was so obsessed with winning England he may have offered the earl one of his daughters in marriage, even though Harold was actually a couple of years older than him; to make it even weirder, Harold apparently chose not the eldest daughter but the second or third, Agatha or Adeliza, who would have been eight or nine. There's no suggestion that Harold wouldn't wait before consummating the marriage, as it was common for children to be betrothed to adults, but it's one of those stories that just looks a bit odd to twenty-first-century readers. In return Harold pledged a sister to one of William's cronies.

It was then that Harold apparently made an oath agreeing that William should be the next king of England, placing his hands inside the duke's in a symbolic gesture of being his vassal. Another Norman story has William making Harold promise to support him as king, and then removing the cloth from the table to show saints' relics underneath, making the promise binding. This was how the Normans presented the story, in order to make William sound clever, although to a later audience it would just make the oath invalid. No one doubted that such an oath, if made, was done under duress. And even if Harold supported William's madcap idea, it's clear the Witan would never support a foreign ruler.

Whether Edward had promised William the throne in 1051, as he claimed, we can never know; there's no real reason to believe that Edward favoured William for being a Norman, since the half-Norman king seemed to hold a grudge against Normandy, as he held a grudge against everyone, for allowing him to rot in virtual poverty and obscurity until his late thirties. Either way, if Edward had nominated Harold on his deathbed then under English custom that overruled any previous promise he had made to William.

Not only was William's claim tenuous, but his plan to invade England was also extremely risky. The Normans were not great seafarers, and William had to build a fleet from scratch, with the sound of metal on wood being heard over the spring and summer of 1066 as forests were cleared to build his fleet. The Norman aristocracy were extremely reluctant to go ahead with the invasion, which they regarded as suicidal. Even if they successfully crossed the sea, which is extremely hazardous, they would be hugely outnumbered in England. Even if they won one battle, victory was still not assured, as another English leader could raise another army. Eventually William tricked the Norman leaders into pledging their support, installing a negotiator who pretended to arbitrate but then presented their agreement as a fait accompli. The price was offering them big chunks of England, which meant already William came not just to claim a crown but to take English land away. It was obviously not going to be popular.

The Church

The Duke of Normandy also had one huge advantage: the support of the Church. This was partly due to military reality, for the Normans now controlled southern Italy and the Roman establishment was therefore keen not to antagonize them. On top of this William had been helped by events in Rome, which was racked by conflict in 1059 between two rival claimants; the duke gave military support to new pope Nicholas II against his rival Benedict X and afterwards Nicholas recognized his marriage.

William was also better at playing politics with a changing Church. Popes, no longer chosen by the German emperor but by cardinals, were getting more powerful and the future Pope Gregory VII, who was plain Cardinal Hildebrand in 1066, wanted kings chosen by popes rather than the other way around. One of the most influential churchmen of the medieval period, Hildebrand to his enemies represented all that was worst in the medieval Church, including the torture of opponents, assassinations and even black magic. But he was also making it less corrupt; up to seven popes in the previous two centuries had been murdered and Roman politics was fantastically violent and Machiavellian, and in 1046 there were three rival popes at the same time.[16] The last one, Benedict IX, had been made pontiff at just twenty and then went on to sell the position, meanwhile being accused of 'many vile adulteries and murders'. All that was changing, and as a sweetener to Hildebrand, the duke now promised he would submit to the rule of the pope after he conquered England, even though this was obviously a lie, and he had absolutely no intention of doing so.

The Church was also becoming stricter about corruption and sexual shenanigans, and was more streamlined, so any signs of deviance in beliefs or habits was clamped down on. William was a skilled diplomat, and his envoy convinced the Pope that the English Church was a hotbed of debauchery and corruption (which, to be fair, it probably was). The English case was not helped by the fact that Stigand, the archbishop of Canterbury, had been excommunicated a number of times and was, in the words of a Flemish biographer, 'irreparably attracted to the devil by riches and worldly glory'.

Likewise Ealdred, the bishop who had previously led an army into Wales, was now both archbishop of York and bishop of Worcester, which 'amusing the simplicity of King Edward' he had acquired 'more by bribery than by reason'.[17]

The Godwins were not so good at diplomacy. Five years earlier Harold had made the mistake of sending his uncouth brother Tostig to Rome to defend the English Church against charges of corruption and general deviancy. Tostig, a half-Viking lout, would not have made a good impression in the refined atmosphere of the Holy See. At Pope Nicholas's Easter get-together Tostig sat next to the pope, but when the Holy Father told Ealdred he'd lose both his bishoprics, Tostig lost his temper and threatened him with nonpayment of the tribute England sent to Rome, called Peter's Pence.

Tostig was only saved on that occasion because on the way home, outside Rome, they were attacked by an outlaw called Gerard, Count of Galeria, and the pontiff was so embarrassed by the lawlessness in his neighborhood he changed his mind.

William was now able to present the invasion as a crusade against the ungodly, even though the Norman church was hardly a paragon of virtue. The king's brother Odo of Bayeux had been made bishop when he was just thirteen and had at least one mistress and a son. Then there was Ivo of Bellême, bishop of Séez, who burned down his own church, he says to get rid of some rough aristocrats who had turned it into a brothel, although this excuse was rejected by Pope Leo.[18] In fact Bishop Bellême's wrongdoings make Stigand look like a comedy antihero in comparison; he murdered his first wife in order to marry the wealthy daughter of a viscount, and during the wedding he attacked his vassal William Giroie, blinding, castrating and mutilating him.

The Bellêmes were even by Norman standards a bad lot. Ivor's niece Mabel, heiress of Bellême, poisoned her brother-in-law and killed many others before she was murdered in her bath by a man she'd taken land from. Her epitaph by a supporter puts it gently: 'a shield of her inheritance, a tower guarding the frontier; to some neighbors dear, to others terrible'.

So badly behaved were the Norman bishops that five of them were forced to attend a conference at Rheims in 1049 to answer charges of corruption. Among them was Geoffrey of Montbray, who was accused of having bought his bishopric; at the council he argued that his brother had bought it without his knowledge, which he swore under oath was true, and was let off. Another bishop present, Malger, was also known to be selling positions in the Church and to have concubines.

But the Normans were much better at playing Church politics, and were more in touch with the growing seriousness of Catholicism, including in areas like priestly celibacy. So with the Pope's blessing, volunteers from across western Europe joined William's crusade, promised either a place in Heaven if they lost or a country estate in England if they won. To further the support of the Church, William now put one of his daughter into a convent.

Having heard the news, William sent Harold a message demanding he hand over the kingdom, and reminding him of their agreement in which one of his cronies would marry Harold's sister and in return Harold marry William's daughter. The king replied that unfortunately he was now married, and that his sister was dead, but if William wanted he could send over her body.[19]

In April 1066 an English spy was captured in Normandy and William sent him back with the words: 'Take this message from me to Harold: he will have nothing to fear from me and can live the rest of his life secure if, within the space of one year, he has not seen me in the place where he thinks his feet are safest.'

CHAPTER EIGHT

The Last Viking

To make things worse, a third ruler now vied for the throne, the Norwegian madman Harald Siguardsson. The six-foot-six-inch Thunderbolt of the North, as he was known, was famed for showing no mercy to his enemies. One of his party tricks was to break a siege by attaching burning wood to the wings of birds, which would then fly back to their nests within the city, starting a fire, a method originally thought up by the Vikings in Russia.[1] At a time when few heads of state fell into the liberal-democratic bracket, Harald's nickname Hardraada—hard ruler—suggests he was not a man to be reasoned with.

Hardraada was the half brother of King Olaf II, the same Olaf who had torn down London Bridge, and might have appeared like something of a monster to his enemies (imagine the Mountain from *Game of Thrones*). Enormously tall and strong, he had blond hair, a long moustache and gigantic hands and feet, and one eyebrow higher than the other. He wore a distinctive mailcoat that went all the way down to his legs to protect his ankles, which his men all called Emma because it looked like a skirt.

Hardraada had inherited the throne from his nephew Magnus, and with it the idea that he should be king of England, a claim that went back to the agreement between Magnus and Hardicnut.

It was all a bit tenuous, but after Hardicnut's unlamented passing Magnus continued to make various threats about invading England without ever bothering to do it; until eventually his death put pay to the idea.

Despite his horrific attachment to violence, Harald was also obsessed with poetry, and saw everything in his life in terms of how it would sound in epic verse. Comparing Viking scald poetry to rap battles might sound like the sort of cringe-worthy analogy a teacher makes to desperately try to impress a class of scary teenagers, but that's basically what it was, a celebration of masculine prowess setting the subject above his peers. What mattered most to Vikings were the songs people would sing about them celebrating their heroic deeds and all-round toughness. Indeed Harald himself wrote a poem, which went like this:

> 'Now I have caused the deaths
> Of thirteen of my enemies
> I kill without compunction
> And remember all my killings
> Treason must be scotched
> By fair means or foul
> Before it overwhelms me
> Oak trees grow from acorns.'

Admittedly it's not Wordsworth, but he did have a sensitive side.

Olaf and Harald's mother Åsta Gudbrandsdatter was a formidable figure. She once told her eldest: 'If I had the choice, I would rather you became king of all Norway, though you lived no longer than Olaf Tryggvason [Olaf I], than that you should remain at the level of Sigurd Syr and die of old age'. Sigurd was Harald's father, who had only remained a petty king; as it is her eldest son did become ruler and reached the ripe old age of forty-two before dying violently in battle.

As a small boy Harald had shown his precocious side. When he and his two brothers were asked what they wanted most in the world, the two older boys replied 'Corn and cattle'. Harald stared intensely and said 'Warriors'.

Harald had grown up during his brother's reign, during which Olaf was mostly in conflict with Norway's aristocrats, who weren't so keen on some of the king's crazy new schemes; in particular Olaf outraged his jarls by his idea of equality before the law. Olaf was overthrown by Canute in 1028 and so reinvaded Norway in 1030 with 2,500 men, among them his fifteen-year-old half brother Harald, twenty-two years younger than him. The battle took place on July 29; the night before, Olaf had had a dream in which a ladder came down from heaven and Jesus beckoned him, which can't have been very encouraging. The next day that particular dream did come true and Olaf was killed in battle.

Afterwards Canute put his mistress/wife Elfgifu in charge of Norway, and so unpopular did she prove that a cult soon grew around the former king, and it is for that reason that the obese warrior became a saint. It didn't help that a famine hit the country and eventually there was a demand to dig up Olaf's remains which turned out to be incorruptible, a sign of sanctity; although Elfgifu tried to explain it away as the result of unusual soil content, her husband's former rival proved more powerful in death than in life.

Harald meanwhile was badly wounded in the battle that had killed his brother and had to hide out in the woods while he tended to his injuries, helped by some local peasants. Afterwards he did what many unemployed Vikings did and took the traditional route up the rivers of Russia towards Constantinople, today's Istanbul, then the capital of the eastern Roman Empire.

The Eastern, or 'Byzantine Empire', didn't collapse in the fifth century like the western half and went on to last another thousand years. Far more advanced than anywhere in the West, its capital was home to perhaps 500,000 people during Harald's time, about half of what it had been a couple of centuries earlier, but still absolutely enormous compared to anywhere in western Europe; Paris had less than 50,000 and London perhaps 15,000 people. Constantinople had street lighting, sewers, drainage, hospitals, 'orphanages, public baths, aqueducts, huge water cisterns, libraries and luxury shops',[2] which to a Viking (or any northern European) would have been mind-blowing. The city had seven palaces, including the Triconchus of Theophilus, which was roofed in gold, and the Sigma, which had fountains flowing with wine. Here the throne of the emperor was guarded by two lions of bronze, in front of which was a metal tree with mechanical birds.

Vikings would sail down the rivers of Russia towards the imperial city, where the north men were employed in the emperor's Varangian guard as mercenaries (their graffiti can still be seen on the upper levels of the Hagia Sophia cathedral, now a museum). Harald became a noted warrior in Byzantium and there are many stories attached to his time there, and some of them may even be true. According to one, he was forced to do battle with a lion in an arena after seducing a noblewoman, but heroically beat the animal. In another story Harald, along with his friends Haldor and Ulf, had to combat a giant snake, and also killed it (there's obviously a bit of a theme here).

One of Harald's other memorable moments came when he gouged out the eyes of the ex-emperor Michael and his uncle Constantine, the losers in one of the empire's internecine squabbles. (Byzantine court coups often ended up with the loser being blinded, or something else awful, although they considered actually killing them a bit excessive.)

Another story involving Harald and his band of Vikings has them besieging an Italian town where they decide to trick some monks into allowing Harald into the city by pretending that he died during the siege, and telling the monks they want to give him a Christian burial, which seems a strikingly unconvincing line (considering a similar story features in Homer, it is literally the oldest trick in the book). Once inside Harald jumped out and he and his men attacked, the saga's recording of the slaughter with the glee of old World War Two comics: 'The monks and other priests who had striven to be the first to receive the corpse now struggled to get away from the Norsemen, who slew everyone round them, clerk or layman, ravaged the town, slaughtered the men, robbed all the churches and loaded themselves with booty'. Awesome!

Harald had eventually returned to Norway loaded with gold, after falling out with the authorities in Constantinople, and bringing back with him a Russian wife. By the time he arrived home his nephew Magnus was on the throne, which Harald now wanted for himself; and Harald was not someone you could reason with. Nephew and uncle had tried ruling jointly for a while, but it had not worked out too well. Tensions got worse when a famous bard, Arnorr Hordarson, was commissioned to recite two songs for the kings in their presence, and it was generally agreed that the one about Magnus was better. Harald was deeply upset.

This was a big deal, for Hardraada had once given Hordarson a spear inlaid with gold, in return for which the skald promised that if he outlived Harald he'd compose a great poem in his honor—which he did, an epic which had as the running refrain 'May the soul of mighty Harald Abide eternally with Christ'. Which seems pretty optimistic.

After Magnus died Harald became sole ruler, acquiring his nickname for his uncomplicated manner of dealing with problems. His main opponent was one Einar Tambarskjelver, 'Wobbly Belly', who led the aristocrats and farmers in opposition to the new king's rule; he once arrived at Harald's court with five hundred warriors and nine warships, as he didn't trust Harald, and rightly so. When eventually some farmers were so unhappy they sent Einar as their representative to take their demands to the king, Harald had Einar hacked to death and then burned all the farmers' houses down. As a poet recalled, 'flames cured the peasants/Of disloyalty to Harold'. Which was true, essentially.

Harald was a great warrior and a flamboyant character, but by the sounds of things quite unhinged, and his total absence of caution would help to bring to an end the great Viking age. And by 1065 he had finally resolved a long-running dispute with Denmark which meant he was free to embark on what would be a totally reckless invasion of England.

Fulford and Stamford Bridge

In the meantime King Harold of England had in the spring gone on a tour of the north to drum up support there. He had been unwell, and had possibly suffered a stroke in the previous two or three years,[3] cured by a German doctor called Adelard who had been sent by the Holy Roman Emperor; Adelard advised Harold to pray at his church at Waltham Cross, which seemed to work.

Harold returned to Westminster from York on April 16, in an atmosphere of increasing paranoia and doom. Many felt that a terrible catastrophe was facing the country, and everyone had their own theories as to why; Bishop Wulfstan of Worcester (nephew of the 'Lupus' Wulfstan from Ethelred's era) suggested that all the nation's problems were down to men not cutting their hair. He believed that men who wore their hair long would be as weak as women and so couldn't defend the country, and all in all seemed quite obsessed with the subject of hair; when men used to go to Wulfstan for Mass whenever they bowed their heads he cut off little bits with a knife he kept with him.

It was at this point that Tostig turned up. Having left England in 1065 he fled to Flanders, his wife's home, and at some point came up with the harebrained idea of invading England. Tostig had spent the spring of 1066 sailing around the North Sea trying to get someone—anyone—to invade with him. First he had tried invading

Lincolnshire by himself but was driven away by Edwin and Morcar and most of his sailors deserted them.

Tostig had then asked his cousin Sweyn Estridsen of Denmark to invade. He said no. Even though Tostig appealed to the king's descent from the Viking Sweyn Forkebeard, father of Canute, Sweyn Estridsen said he knew he couldn't win, which was hardly the old Viking spirit, and Tostig then taunted him with cowardice— but that didn't work either. However Sweyn was so alarmed at the prospect of either Harald Hardraada or Duke William becoming king of England that he sent troops to Harold instead; there were most likely Danes on the English side at Hastings.

Tostig might also have been rebuffed in Flanders and Normandy, but the king of Norway agreed, and an invasion plan was launched, one that in retrospect seems astonishingly unwise. At the time Norway was cut off from the rest of Europe, so Harald didn't know much about the internal politics of England, in the way the leaders of Denmark or Flanders would have, specifically that everyone in England hated Tostig, apart from maybe his sister. The plan was entirely reckless, and some of Harald's actions suggest he didn't think he was coming back; perhaps he just thought the whole adventure would make a good poem one day, and that's all that mattered. As for Tostig, his behavior at the time is the most puzzling, so some historians think the only logical explanation is that he had gone insane.

Harald was a superstitious man, and before setting sail he went to the tomb of St Olaf, unlocked it, clipped his nails and hair, an old Viking custom, locked the tomb and threw the keys in the river. Before they set off there were lots of nightmares and omens among the Vikings. Hardraada apparently dreamed of his brother, who warned him there was a difference between an honorable death fighting for a birthright, and falling in battle trying to take from someone else, and telling him this whole expedition would end badly. One of Harald's sidekicks, Gyrd, also had a nightmare, where he saw an English army led by a huge troll woman riding a wolf which had a man's body in its jaw and blood in the corner of its mouth. And after it ate the man, the troll-woman consumed them all. Which was either a sign of doom, or that he'd been drinking far too much. Despite all this Harald seemed to treat the thing as any good Viking should, as one big adventure.

They first sailed to the Shetlands and Orkneys, where Harald left one of his wives, which suggests he may have not expected to come home and wanted this one safe away from his other wife (like most Viking rulers, he hadn't entirely conformed to Christian rules just yet). There some dynastic marriages were arranged with the local Viking rulers, and the fleet headed south, with some Orcadians joining the expedition.

In fact once this all started everyone began claiming the throne of England. Conan of Brittany now threw his hat in, on some spurious grounds; however he ended up mysteriously dying from poisoning later in the year.

The English army, or *fyrd*, had spent the summer guarding the south coast, waiting for the Normans to arrive, but as September went on the chances of invasion were starting to fade, since the sea would get too rough to cross. The big problem with an army made up of farmers was that if they didn't return home in time the crops would rot and they'd starve.

On September 8, thinking it was getting too late for the Normans to cross, Harold sent the army home. A few days later he returned to London with a huge pain in his leg, and two days afterwards was told that the Norwegians had landed in Northumbria and burned down Scarborough, a town on the Yorkshire coast.[4] Harald had built a large bonfire at the top of the hill there, and then pushed it all down onto the roofs of houses below, setting fire to it. As one historian explained: 'There was really not much point in it, except that it was fun'.[5]

In Yorkshire the invading army was met by a pitiful English force led by Edwin and Morcar at a village called Fulford, easily beating them; after the battle the invaders walked over English heads lying in the river 'like stepping stones'. Had the northern earls more faith in the king they might have retreated behind the nearby walls of York, but they did not expect help so soon, Harold's army being in the south.

Tostig had told all the Norwegians he was really popular in York, but when they arrived Harald found that his English ally was in fact hated by everyone. In the city not a single person came out to greet the former earl, so the invaders left and went back to their base in nearby Riccall for a celebration. They expected that it would be many days, if not weeks, before King Harold arrived.

In fact the English army was marching along Roman roads at speed and on September 24, as York surrendered, Godwinson was only a day's hike away. The following day the second battle of the year took place. The Vikings were so confident they wouldn't face opposition that they walked to Stamford Bridge without their mail coats and just wore shirts, expecting to arrive in the village to be given money and hostages. They were in merry mood, but when they arrived saw a large body of men meeting them. Tostig, deluded as always, assumed they were coming to surrender, until it dawned on them that the southern army had reached them in record time, covering up to fifty miles a day.

Before the two sides fought there was a dramatic meeting between the Godwinson brothers. Much of this story comes down to us from a fourteenth-century Icelandic saga, *Hemings þáttr*, which draws on older Norwegian stories, and Norse tales often feature brothers who are deadly rivals.[6] In the story Harold pretends to be a messenger from the English leader, and approaches the Norwegians where, spotting his brother, 'a big strong man, and a man of many words,'[7] calls out in English that King Harold offers him a third of his kingdom if he changes sides. Tostig replies that he could not desert Hardraada and asked what he could offer the Norwegian king. Harold replies: 'Since he was not content with his own kingdom, I'll give him six feet of English ground—a little more, perhaps, since he's a tall man. But nothing more than that, since I don't care about him.'

Tostig refuses this offer, and his brother departs. Only afterwards does Hardraada learn who the messenger is, and is angered because his enemy had been in arrow's range. As it was, Harald would soon have seven feet of ground, and the Viking age was going to come to a very abrupt end. The next the world hears about Norwegians they're handing out peace prizes.

Before the battle Hardraada was thrown from his horse while reviewing troops, a bad portent, but when the English tried to cross the bridge they were held up by one enormous Viking who stood firm and defended it single-handedly, killing as many as forty English soldiers, until he was speared from below by an Englishman who had sneaked under the bridge. The saga has the defenders apologizing for this discourteous way of killing the enemy, which seems very British.

After the shield wall was broken Harald launched into a trademark Viking *berserker* fury, where one man almost in a state of supernatural possession would charge forward to attack the enemy—except that he was immediately killed with an arrow in the windpipe, a rather anticlimactic ending.

As he lay dying and the English came at him Harald, almost absurdly, dictated a poem to his scribe to be recorded for posterity, at least it was claimed by a saga writer, his last words being: 'We march forward in battle-array without our corselets to meet the dark blades: helmets shine but I have not mine, for now our armor lies down on the ships.'

With the Norwegians leaderless, Tostig continued the fight until he, too, was killed, according to the sagas with an arrow in the eye (this may have been medieval historians getting confused with the story about Harold's death three weeks later). Harold solemnly buried his brother at York Minster, and magnanimously allowed the surviving Scandinavians to go home, the pitiful band filling only twenty or so ships out of three hundred; a visitor to the area in the 1120s recalled that there was still a mountain of bones visible on the battle site.[8] Among the survivors were Harald's sons Magnus and Olaf, who also took with them Tostig's young boys. One of Harald's men, Styrkar, got away and came upon an English carter wearing a coat. He offered to buy it, but the man taunted him for losing the battle, so Styrkar cut his head off. The moral of the story: if a mad Vikings makes a decent offer, accept it.

Although no one knew it, Stamford Bridge represented the end of the Viking age. The losses would have taken Norway a long time to recover from, and as Christianity became more firmly established and Scandinavian states more centralized the likes of Harald Hardraada became a thing of the past.

Harold Godwinson had won one of the most decisive battles of the medieval era; unfortunately it wasn't to be even the most important battle that year. On September 28 the Normans landed in Sussex, and Harold would have heard the news four or five days later, most likely while already heading south with his exhausted army. What a year it was turning out to be.

CHAPTER NINE

The Battle of Hastings

Villiam's invasion fleet comprised between seven hundred and a thousand boats[1] and was led by his fifty-five-foot flagship, a gift from his wife which featured on its masthead the leopard of Normandy. The duke brought with him mercenaries from Flanders, Germany, Italy, Denmark, Brittany and France, but it wasn't all plain sailing—he fell flat on his face as he jumped ashore on English soil; an underling immediately proclaimed that the duke was embracing his new kingdom.[2] This was after two of the ships had already been lost at sea, one of which contained the fleet's official clairvoyant. 'Not much of a soothsayer,' William muttered when he was told, 'couldn't foretell his own end.'

Back in London, Harold's brother Gyrth made the sensible suggestion that the king should defend the city while he met the invaders, so that even his defeat and death would not mean the end of the kingdom; when Harold's mother tried to stop him going to fight William 'he insolently kicked her'. Harold, out of pride or over-confidence, felt he had to lead his army, and protect his homeland.

The invaders had begun plundering the land in Sussex and terrorizing its inhabitants, a deliberate attempt to provoke the king to come out and fight—and it worked.[3] Harold's family came from Sussex and he may have felt that to allow a foreign army to go around his home county unmolested would make him a failure; had Harold waited he could have had an army twice or three times the size. The king had also suffered a number of desertions from his *fyrd* after Stamford Bridge, largely it is thought because he refused to let them keep enemy plunder.

And so all of England's leaders went off to Hastings, except Edgar Atheling, who was all of thirteen. Had Harold listened to his mother then, even an English defeat at Hastings would mean the Normans having to face another battle against a fresh English force, which could draw more men from around the countryside, and their numbers would inevitably be depleted by diseases of various kind. In fact, so much of the Norman conquest was avoidable if Harold had been a bit more cautious.

By the evening of October 13 the two armies were both camped near Hastings and the English, despite their exhaustion, had the advantage in that Harold had found higher ground on a spot called Senlac. William ordered for an attack in the morning, despite the disadvantages of charging uphill.

Norman chroniclers later claimed that the English had spent the evening getting drunk long into the night, as if anyone would have thought the eve of battle was a great time to have a blowout. One said the English 'as we have heard passed the night without sleep, in drinking and singing . . . the Normans passed the whole night in confessing their sins, and received the sacrament.'[4]

The Norman poet Wace went even further: 'All the night they ate and drank, and never lay down on their beds. They might be seen carousing, gambolling and dancing and singing' while the Normans 'betook themselves all night to their orisons, and were in very serious mood'. The Normans liked to paint the English as mindless drunks which, to be fair, they were, but also history is recorded by monks, who always presented any losing side as debauched, to enforce the message that good things come to those who pray.

From nine a.m.[5] some seven to eight thousand Englishmen went into battle against a similar number of invaders, the English shouting *Ut!* (Out!) and the enemy *Dex Aie!* (with God's Help!). The English were formed in very tight lines, with the men of Kent at the front and the 'settled Danes' of Yorkshire on the left; the men of London stood at the centre, around King Harold and his battle standard of the Wessex dragon, the wyvern, as well as his personal banner, the 'Fighting Man'. Facing them the invaders were formed into three groups, with Bretons on the left, Normans in the centre, and French on the right.

The English army featured three thousand of the elite house-carls, each carrying an enormous two-handed axe that could chop a horse in half. However the English were on foot, while in contrast the Normans had two thousand cavalry, and one thousand archers—far more than the defenders brought. The fighting went on for most of the day, unusual when battles were usually finished within an hour (indeed pitched battles were rare in this period, as armies tended to try to avoid it in the hope that the other side would go home).

William wore around his neck the relics that Harold supposedly swore on, trying to goad his men to fight, but being Normans they were goaded enough. The duke gave an eve of battle speech to his men and 'the knights were so excited that they rushed impetuously off before he had finished and left him speaking alone'. Then William put his mail coat on backwards, again seen as a bad omen—but then such bad omens are common in stories.

Before the battle proper, Duke William called for a knight to take on a Saxon in one-to-one combat, a suicide mission, which was taken up by Taillefer, who was not just a military adventurer but also a professional juggler. He killed the Saxon who challenged him and then charged at their shield wall, being killed instantly, and rather predictably.

The battle began with the Normans firing a volley of arrows aimed at the faces of the opposition; few of them made any impact on the heavily-protected housecarls, and so the invaders tried wave after wave of attacks. Duke William was so involved in the fighting he had three horses cut from below him during the day.

Things could have gone either way; at one point rumors spread that the duke was dead, and William threw back his helmet to show his men otherwise. At this point they were on the verge of panic, and he shouted at them that if they fled they would all die.

The Normans charged and charged, but there was deadlock. At one point the Bretons on the left side began a retreat and, thinking that the enemy were in tatters, the English chased them and broke formation. This gave the Normans the idea of feigning a retreat and when they did so again the English lost their formation and the high ground, and Harold's brothers Gyrth and Leofwine were killed.

Now William ordered four knights to go after the king, who hacked him to death, the first stabbing him in the chest, two more attacking his head and arms, before the last knight cut off his leg, or possibly his genitals. According to one account William thought this action was a bit excessive even for his standards and he sent the offending soldier home without any reward.[6] Emasculation was surprisingly common, even though it was seen as rather beyond the pale.

Harold may or may not have been hit in the eye: the story first appears one hundred years later, and the arrow shaft on the famous Bayeux Tapestry may have been only added in the eighteenth century by bored nuns. It's possible also that the eye story was Norman propaganda, since blinding was the biblical punishment for oath-breakers; but either way he was dead. One story has William leading this death squad but it is extremely unlikely he'd have done something so risky; likewise with a later tale that Gyrth unhorsed William before the duke killed him, which is most likely borrowed from *The Iliad*.

By the end of the day the Normans had lost 2,500 men, the English 4,000, including most of the country's nobility. After the battle William didn't bother to bury the defeated, and it was left to Harold's mistress, Edith Swan-Neck, to identify him by a part 'known only to her', as his face had been so badly mutilated. However the indignity continued; William wouldn't give up the body, even after Harold's mother offered him her son's weight in gold if she'd return him, and to this day no one knows where England's last English king lies. One story has William giving him an ironic headstone on the shore to guard England from invasion, the deed carried out by William Malet,[7] one of nineteen 'companions' of the duke who can be identified with certainty. [8] There were also legends of Harold surviving the battle and becoming a sort of wandering hermit.[9]

The site of the battle is marked by a derelict monastery, built after the fight in thanksgiving by the victor in the hope that perhaps God might overlook the thousands of people he'd killed in the conquest. The pope had insisted they build it as a condition of his support for the morally dubious invasion, and William put up the high altar on the spot where Harold was struck dead, dedicating the church to St Martin, patron saint of soldiers and alcoholics. The monastery was destroyed in the Reformation, but is today open to the public, thousands of whom visit every day.[10]

Afterwards the Normans lost many men chasing the surviving Saxons into an area where they died in an 'evil ditch', the *malfosse* as they called it. The invaders also believed a fresh English army was arriving in the morning: they had not yet won the kingdom, and in London the thirteen-year-old Edgar was hastily declared king. William's army now went from town to town, and after a few atrocities Dover surrendered to them; England at the time had only twelve quite basic castles, and so was unable to do much against an army like this. Then in Canterbury William got dysentery and could have died, in which case the whole expedition would still have been a waste of time. However he recovered and after they circled London and rampaged to the west, Archbishop Ealdred of York submitted at Wallingford on the Thames; soon Edgar, the bishops and the other leading men accepted William as king.

On Christmas Day 1066 the monumentally expensive Westminster Abbey started paying its way when William was crowned king of England in a service said in English and French. The native crowd, keen to have no trouble with their new overlords, cheered him sycophantically with cries of '*Vivat Rex*'—Long Live the King. William's nervous, trigger-happy army mistook the insincere cheers for an uprising and fired on the crowd, before setting fire to the surrounding buildings. It was not a good start, PR wise, and it was not going to get any better. The *Anglo-Saxon Chronicle* groaned: 'They built castles far and wide throughout the land, oppressing the unhappy people, and things went ever from bad to worse.'

The Tapestry

Much of what we know about the Battle of Hastings comes from possibly the first comic book in history, known as the Bayeux Tapestry although strictly speaking it's an embroidery. It tells the story from Harold's visit of 1064 to the battle itself, with Latin text above the pictures, and was made soon after—although it lay hidden in the cathedral in Bayeux until discovered in the 1720s.

The tapestry is only nine inches tall but eighty yards long, that is a third longer than Nelson's column,[11] or just under half that of the Washington Memorial, although rather frustratingly the last few bits may have been ripped off; it ends with Harold being killed and the English running away.

It was most likely made by Kentish weavers at the instigation of a leading Norman but it's not explicitly pro-William. Although it shows Harold swearing to uphold William's claim, the Normans are also presented burning down a village and it refers to Harold as 'king', something the Normans refused to recognize.

The tapestry is strange in many ways—running above and below the main narrative are a series of figures, including strange beasts and the 'odd erotic incident'.[12] In the scene where William takes Harold to the hall in Rouen, below them is shown a naked man wielding a tool and working on a wooden object which could be a coffin. It also features some characters we know nothing about, including a dwarf called Turold and a woman, Ælfgifu, who appears with a priest placing a veil on her; beneath them is a naked man with an erection mimicking the priest's action. It's some sort of in-joke.

But the tapestry also created a bit of confusion about the events; for centuries the keepers cut off bits and gave them away as souvenirs[13] and so no one is entirely sure how accurate it is now. It is still not clear which figure is the king under the words 'Harold is killed', and whether it was some other poor fellow who was shown being hit in the eye, or if this was added later.

It's thought the tapestry was commissioned by Bishop Odo, because it was probably made in Kent, which after 1066 he owned in its entirety. Odo is barely mentioned in any written reports of the battles, but he is a major figure in the tapestry; only William and Harold appear more often.

Another alternative theory is that it was ordered by Eustace of Boulogne, the Confessor's brother-in-law who had joined the invasion despite being hostile to William, who previously killed his stepson Walter of Maine. When Eustace joined, William took his son Eustace hostage and the two men would later fall out. Of the two written accounts of the battle, one shows Eustace as a central figure who leads besides William, and another as an abject coward who only survives because he is knocked unconscious.

Alternatively Harold's sister Edith may have commissioned the tapestry; she is only one of three women to appear in it, out of 626 people, and is portrayed positively. After Hastings she was allowed to live out the rest of her miserable life in peace, and when she died in 1075 William paid for a lavish funeral, perhaps the least he could have done after killing three of her brothers and having another kept in a dungeon for thirty years.

We're lucky to still have the tapestry at all, as it was almost destroyed in 1792 during the French Revolution when it was going to be cut up in order to cover an ammunition wagon. Then some revolutionaries planned to rip it to pieces and use as confetti as part of some demented 'festival of reason', before a courageous official prevented them. The tapestry became famous soon after this when Napoleon became interested in it, seeing as it portrayed a successful conquest of England. He had it brought to Paris and a play appeared around that time about William's wife making it (in France it is known as The Tapestry of Queen Matilda, after a mistaken belief she was behind it).

When a sort of comet appeared in 1803 it was seen as a sign, and although Napoleon had 150 to 200,000 soldiers and 2,000 ships ready for an invasion it never worked out this time. Interest in the tapestry continued to grow and in 1816 Charles Stothard, a draughtsman for the Society of Antiquaries in London was commissioned to make drawings and write a commentary over two years. This he did; he also stole a bit and took it home, this chunk ending up with the Victoria and Albert Museum who handed it back in 1871 (however by that stage the bit had been replaced so it was never sown back in). Another part was stolen by a vicar, the Rev Thomas Frognall Dibdin, in 1842.

Meanwhile some Victorian ladies, led by one Mrs Elizabeth Wardle, wanted England to have a version of the tapestry so they got together and made an almost exact replica. However because sexual mores had changed somewhat in eight centuries one of the naked men had his genitals removed in the new version, and the other had some underpants helpfully put on. The otherwise-perfect replica is still on display in Reading.

CHAPTER TEN

The Norman Yoke

The country was now under the rule of a foreign elite; the Witan would disappear forever, the Church purged of English bishops and English cults, shires were renamed counties, and 'Gyrth' and 'Leofwine' became the kind of names you only gave your kids if you actively wished them to get beaten up at school.

Every Englishman who fought at Hastings whether he live or died, had his land confiscated afterwards, a taste of things to come; William ordered the abbot of Bury to hand over everything in his area owned by men 'who stood against me in battle and were slain there'.[1] The English elite were purged, exiled and driven from their homes, and within a generation there would be no native aristocracy left.

Straight after Christmas the Normans began work on the Tower of London, and then they would build five hundred castles in fifty years, roughly one every ten miles, of which ninety were stone.[2] These fortresses were not just symbols of occupation, but an eyesore for anyone living in the overwhelmingly one-storey buildings nearby, many of whom were also forced into building them.

The *Chronicle* recorded that after 1066: 'When the castles were built, they filled them with devils and wicked men . . . they levied taxes on the villages . . . they robbed and burned'. Women were subject to the sort of horrors one expects, as the *Chronicle* recorded: 'noble maidens were exposed to the insults of low-born soldiers, and lamented their dishonoring by the scum of the earth'.

The native aristocracy were dispossessed if they weren't already dead; five thousand thegns (the equivalent of knights) disappeared as a class, and between a third and half of the country was shared out between just 170 Norman barons; thousands of previously free natives were reduced to serfdom.

There were as many as 200,000 Norman and French settlers in England, but more likely closer to 20,000, out of a total population of maybe two million. Many of the leading barons in England now were Bretons rather than Normans, and others Parisian French. In fact the English referred to the conquerors as 'French', and sometimes 'Romans', as this is what French speakers still called themselves.[3]

William spent the winter of 1066 in England while his wife ran Normandy, and when he and his cronies returned to France in the spring the Parisians were 'dazzled by the beauty of their clothing, which was embroidered with gold'. The new Norman elite were vastly wealthy; according to a 2000 *Sunday Times* estimate Bishop Odo, who was given Kent and land in twenty-two counties, was worth £43.2 billion ($52 billion) in today's money, which would put him ahead of the most rapacious third world kleptocrat. William's other half brother, Robert of Mortain, was worth £46.1 billion ($56 billion) while William of Warenne a staggering £57.6 billion ($71 billion); he held lands in thirteen counties. The new king was richer still, but despite William being staggeringly wealthy, the Godwin family had been probably even richer than he was.

Another crony, William Fitzosbern, as well as being made Earl of Hereford, got the Isle of Wight, where he immediately began building a castle. Unfortunately he was killed only five years later after a Flemish countess had offered to marry him if he invaded her county; that kind of offer was irresistible to a Norman. Even William's cook Tezelin got a whole manor, Addington in Surrey, after making the king a particularly delicious soup, of chicken, almond, milk and capons.[4]

The Church was also dominated by Normans, who deliberately suppressed the veneration of English saints and undermined native Christianity. At Glastonbury Abbey in 1083 when English monks there resisted a new Norman liturgy, soldiers killed or wounded several of the brothers, firing arrows at them from choir loft. The *Chronicle* recorded: 'blood came down from the altar onto the steps and from the steps to the floor'.

The new super-elite, who each had enough land and money to run a small army, became the basis of the feudal system, from the Latin for 'payment' or 'obligation', under which the lords owed the king certain duties in return for holding their land and passing it onto their heirs. Although traditionally the Normans were blamed for introducing 'feudalism', something fairly similar existed already.[5]

In England south of the Tees just two Englishmen, Thurkill of Arden and Colswein of Lincoln, were holding baronial estates in 1086. Although the Anglo-Saxons had an aristocracy their Norman replacements were far smaller in number and far richer; so Roger de Busli held land in Nottinghamshire and south Yorkshire that had previously belonged to eighty different English landowners.

Huge areas were set aside as 'forests', one-third of the country, the word literally meaning royal lands rather than a wooded place, where the commoners weren't allowed to hunt, the New Forest being the most famous (the whole of Essex was also a forest). Punishment for hunting on these royal lands was severe. Any man caught poaching would have his hamstring pulled and be crippled for life; they applied the same punishment to any dog found doing the same. In fact any dog even living in the royal forests had to have three claws cut off on each front paw, and by the reign of Richard I (1189–1199), the deer in royal forests were tame.

Like many homicidal maniacs, King William was sentimental about animals, and 'loved deer like he was their father', as one chronicler put it (although to be fair he hated his own son).

Peasants were evicted for the sake of hunting and bystanders were obliged to provide passing hunts with refreshments—otherwise they could be charged with treason. It is argued that whereas previously hunting had been a classless pastime, as it remains elsewhere in Europe, in England it became seen as an upper-class sport, and in the New Forest numerous peasants were evicted to make way for the hunting grounds.[6] The Normans were so obsessed with the sport they introduced pheasants and rabbits into Britain for the express purpose of killing them.

There was always going to be conflict, which is why William banned his men from drinking in taverns to stop fights. However the Normans were in a state of permanent alarm at the natives, so a system was introduced—The Laws of Englishry—that any body found by the authorities was assumed to be a Norman murdered by the English unless otherwise proven, and led to the nearest village paying a massive fine (if it turned out to be an Englishman, they were okay). The unintended consequence of this would be that murder would go from being a private matter settled by fine (as the Saxons treated it) to being a crime against the crown itself, but at the time this quite progressive idea was not the intention.

The Resistance

After returning to Normandy in 1067 William left his brother Odo in charge, but it wasn't long before he was back dealing with rebellion. The first actually came from one of his own allies, Eustace of Boulogne, who in 1067 led an uprising in, of all places, Dover, claiming now to be its defender. Eustace, a descendent of Alfred the Great and Charlemagne, perhaps wanted to be king himself, and then invaded East Anglia with two hundred ships, but his Danish ally Sweyn was paid off and deserted him; Eustace, an undeservingly lucky man, escaped with an apology to the king.

The remnants of the Godwinson family, now living in Ireland, also appeared on the scene again. Harold's son Godwin launched an invasion of the West Country but it fizzled out and he went back across the sea. Harold's mother Gytha, well into her sixties, led a far more dangerous rebellion in Exeter, which lasted eighteen days and cost several hundred lives. The tough old lady then fled the country, probably to Scandinavia.

William marched into Exeter in December 1067 with an army of Norman and English soldiers. Although he was normally ferocious, he had not allowed plundering in the city after it had surrendered and had not increased the taxes it had to pay. And so when in 1069 a rising broke out in Devon and Cornwall Exeter sided with William.

There was also the eccentric Eadric the Wild, who led a brief uprising in the border area with Wales, and claimed to have married a fairy princess and introduced her to William with 'beauty, say hello to beast' (William never confirmed the story).

But the most serious opposition, and most brutally punished, took place in the north. At first William had given the job of running Northumbria to Tostig's former sidekick Copsi, but he was murdered after only five weeks, killed in an ambush by one Oswulf, son of Eadwulf of Bernicia; then in the autumn Oswulf was himself killed by a brigand. His cousin Gospatric then bought the earldom from William.

The uprising began in 1069 when a member of the old murder-happy Northumbrian royal family slew a Norman appointee, and a combined English and Danish army marched on York and brutally killed almost all the Normans. Two escaped and brought the news back to William.

The retribution was predictably brutal. After William's 'Harrying of the North', in which cattle and corn were burned and thousands slaughtered, several villages and whole districts ceased to exist altogether. As many as 150,000 were killed, and the survivors left so desolate that they resorted to cannibalism; Yorkshire lost three-quarters of its population and the north of England didn't recover for centuries. Pious as always, William insisted on celebrating the nativity while campaigning in York in 1069, in a town smouldering with ruin. Even Simeon of Durham, William's propagandist, could not justify this destruction: 'I would rather lament the griefs and sufferings of the wretched people than make a vain attempt to flatter the perpetrator of such infamy'.

Another, more celebrated heroic stand came with the mysterious Hereward the Wake, a minor nobleman from Lincolnshire, who led an uprising with the help of his trusty sword, 'Brainbiter'. Hereward was joined by Earls Morcar and Edwin, the latter peeved because he had been promised William's daughter Adeliza in marriage but the king changed his mind after four years of waiting.

However in 1071 Edwin was betrayed by his own men, who cut his head off and brought it to William. Even William thought this was a bit much, and was 'so horrified upon seeing the grisly spectacle that he was moved to tears'.[7] Poor Adeliza, who was heartbroken after the marriage to Harold had not worked out, wasn't having much luck with her engagements. After a third, to Alfonso of Castile, ended in failure she eschewed all further talk of marriage and entered a nunnery.'[8]

Although celebrated as a hero, Hereward's claim to be a freedom fighter is slightly colored by the sacking of the Abbey at Peterborough, which was English owned. The *Chronicle* reported dryly that 'they said he did it out of loyalty to his minster'. Hereward was promised help from the Danes—the Normans must have been pretty bad if people were getting nostalgic about the Vikings—and indeed the Danes were welcomed to Peterborough in 1070, but then they just went off with the abbey treasure.

Hereward's forces were besieged and beaten, though he disappeared into the night, leading to speculation that a) he never died and will continue the fight until England is free or b) he just drowned. King William's grand survey of England, the Domesday Book, later records a Hereward living in the West Midlands years later, and some historians think it the same man, though it seems unlikely a notorious outlaw, except a really stupid one, would give his real name on a census form.

The various uprisings only served to make Norman domination more brutal. The king had initially tried to learn English and rule in a conciliatory way, but he gave up on the language and after 1070 English no longer appeared on official documents. From now on he would rule with terror alone.

One thing that can be said about the Normans is that they were generally quite sparing in their use of execution, and William only beheaded one English aristocrat during his reign, the Northumbrian Waltheof, in 1076. He had been part of the 1069 uprising in York but had made peace with the king and married his niece Judith, and even been made Earl of Northumbria after William had exiled his cousin Gospatric. However despite the conflict with the Normans Waltheof and his relatives were still busily engaged in blood feuds with other northerners over ancient disputes, the main one involving a family that had murdered his great-grandfather, Uhtred the Bold.

Despite being let off once Waltheof went on to join a conspiracy with two Norman aristocrats, Ralph the Breton and William Fitzosbern, who rebelled because the king refused them permission to marry the women of their choice. Waltheof and his two allies, according to Orderic, spread the message that 'the man who calls himself king is unworthy, since he is a bastard . . . He unjustly invaded the fair kingdom of England and unjustly slew his true heirs . . . all men hate him and his death would cause great rejoicing.' Which was probably true. However the game was given away when Waltheof was accused of conspiracy by his own wife, Judith, and was condemned to death.

He started crying during his recitation of the Lord's prayer and the executioner, impatient, cut off his head. It was said that his head continued to recite 'but deliver us from evil, Amen'. Ralph the Breton was put in prison where William sent him some gifts; he foolishly burned them, and so was never released.

The Vikings still tried to invade a couple of times, but they had lost their old sparkle. King Sweyn had died in 1074 and there was a struggle between his sons Harold and Canute; Canute, the loser, sailed to England with two hundred warships and although William took it seriously, and Durham and other castles were garrisoned, the Danes just attacked York Minster and then ran off home. Meanwhile the locals had taken the opportunity to murder some Normans, and so Bishop Odo led an army for some more harrying.

In 1085 Canute, now king of Denmark, raised a coalition to overthrow William once again. He assembled a fleet but there was a dispute with his own subjects and the ships sailed off without him; the following year he was murdered by his own people. Still, it didn't end there for Canute because eventually he ended up as a saint, on some fairly spurious grounds, mostly that there was a crop failure soon after his death which was attributed to divine punishment.

However Canute's threat led the king to do something which historians are eternally grateful for, conducting a huge survey of every piece of private property in the country. The idea was to find out how much everyone owned so he could raise a new tax to fight off the Danish invasion. The authorities called it the King's Roll, or the Winchester Book, but the natives, fighting conquest with irony (not very successfully), named it The Domesday Book, as if it was the very day of judgement from the Lord.[9] The book recorded who owned what in 1086, when it was made, and who owned it on the 'day King Edward lived and died', and the speed in which it was made is seen as proof of how efficient the Anglo-Saxon state was; it was so extensive that it was last used to settle a land dispute in the early twentieth century.[10]

As for Edgar the Atheling, he had been involved in the 1069 uprising, or at least been a figurehead, before fleeing to Scotland where his sister married King Malcolm. The Scots ruler had promised to help Edgar regain the throne but this was always going to be not entirely popular with the English who feared the Scots at least as much as the Normans.

Instead William invaded Scotland and Malcolm recognized he was in fact right; Edgar had now wandered around the continent with the king of France promising to help him if he'd invade Normandy, but this failed, too. Eventually Malcolm persuaded his brother-in-law to make peace with William, after which he seems to have been quite a lowly figure, and the Domesday Book shows his estate worth just £10. Eventually in 1086 William allowed Edgar to go to Apulia in southern Italy with two hundred knights to fight with the Normans there.

After all opposition was crushed, the Normans responded to resistance with increased fines. England now groaned under the weight of taxes to support the conquering army, and William still imposed Danegeld, even though it was as outdated as asking the taxpayers now to pay for a fund to fight Hitler.[11]

The Normans: mass murderers and also sexist

Another way in which Normans are depicted as baddies is that they were puritanical male chauvinists who oppressed women. Some historians argue that women had more rights in Anglo-Saxon England than they did at any time until even Victorian times. Before 1066 there were strict penalties for sexual assaults and rape, whether against free women or slaves, and for fraud, impotence or enslavement a woman could have a marriage annulled and keep all her goods. As far back as the laws of King Ethelbert (written soon after AD 600) women could walk out of a marriage and take half the property, and a third of the thirty surviving wills from Anglo-Saxon England are from females. Before the Normans, as well as owning property or running monasteries, women could hold the position of' 'lord', literally 'loaf-giver', a title not exclusive to men. Husbands were also expected to endow their wives with a cash payment to secure their financial independence, the *morgengifu*—literally 'morning gift', paid by a man to his new wife on the morning after their first wedding night—on condition that she had had sex with him the night before, which must have made her feel really good about the whole thing.

There were also double monasteries in the seventh and eighth centuries ruled over by abbesses who were not under the control of men, something that would have been inconceivable to the later Church. Attitudes can also be guessed at from surviving literature; in the Anglo-Saxon poem *Genesis B*, Eve is not the cause of man's downfall but was being tricked by the devil's heavenly vision.

Generally historians agree that life was better for women in Anglo-Saxon England than in the following centuries, and like the Vikings they had a fairly progressive view. Progressive for the period that is. However some others dispute this image of the Normans as proto–golf club chauvinists, and claim that women could still have wills and contracts, hold land, sue and appear as their own attorney before the law. Some say it was all a myth invented by a mixture of nineteenth-century feminists and Francophobes and that the condition of women didn't actually change that much.

One woman who certainly did well out of the conquest was Matilda, William's wife, who ran a number of religious houses and received countless rents and gifts; London had to provide oil for her lamps and wood, while Norwich had to give her a small horse each year.[12]

The Normans were certainly progressive in a couple of ways, though; during William's reign the death penalty was abolished, since the Normans didn't approve of execution, although his son reintroduced it. Instead wrongdoers were usually castrated and blinded, which was progress of sorts (blinding was biblically significant and the king, a very religious man in some ways, was obsessed with swearing eye-related oaths and apparently coined the phrase 'damn your eyes').

The Norman conquest would also embed chivalry, the warrior code which in England reached its high point in the fourteenth century, and which prohibited the killing or mistreatment of aristocratic prisoners, who in Anglo-Saxon times would have expected to be executed.[13] After Waltheof no English aristocrat would be beheaded until the fourteenth century. Chivalry also encompassed ideas about the treatment of women, and although much of what we imagine by chivalry today is a later romantic idea from the far gentler Victorian era, as the medieval period went on women and children were increasingly spared during war.

Although he increased the number of serfs in England, William did phase out slavery, under pressure from the Church, and there was a big difference; although serfs were not free, unlike slaves they couldn't be legally killed without good reason, and because they were tied to the land their families weren't split up. Going from slavery to serfdom was a big improvement.

There were other positive aspects to Norman rule, such as the continental influences it brought on the English Church. Having become friends eventually, William had hired the Italian Abbot Lanfranc to replace Stigand as archbishop of Canterbury, largely against his will it has to be said. Lanfranc was one of the greatest minds of his time, if also one of the most modest. He had served for twenty years as head of Bec Abbey in Normandy, and despite being widely respected had refused many prestigious jobs because he wanted to stay in the monastery; he was either very holy, or lazy. Popes Nicholas II and Alexander II offered him a place in the curia—the Vatican bureaucracy—but he refused, and in 1067 turned down the plum job of archbishop of Rouen. But William made him an offer he couldn't refuse. Under the Normans the number of English monasteries, which were at the time the equivalent both to universities and industry, increased, from 60 in 1066 to between 250 and 300 in 1154.[14] In particular the white monks from Abbey of Citeaux, known as Cistercians, would become famed sheep farmers across the north, growing very rich.[15]

By all accounts Lanfranc absolutely hated living in England, and complained: 'I am continually hearing, seeing and experiencing so much unrest among different people, such distress and injuries, such hardness of heart, greed and dishonesty, such a decline in holy Church, that I am weary of my life.' A few weeks after becoming head of the English Church he had written to the pope trying to get out by saying he was inadequate. The pope refused.

There were other positives to Norman rule. Arguably the conquest made central authority in England stronger, and the country never had the same fracturing as in Germany or France, which would lead to continual war and despotism, although geography meant it was probably going that way anyhow.[16]

The Normans also put up many great buildings: Winchester Cathedral was the longest in western Europe, the Tower of London the biggest keep and Westminster Great Hall the largest secular covered space; Christ Church priory in Canterbury probably took more cut stone than the pyramids.[17] The Normans introduced the Romanesque style of stone building to England, where previously most had been wooden. On the other hand quite a lot of Norman buildings fell down—churches at Winchester, Ely, Evesham, Bury St Edmunds and Chichester all collapsed shortly after their hasty construction, and the Normans also knocked down many Anglo-Saxon churches.

There are also numerous beautiful small churches directly linked to the bloodshed of 1066; the Church ordered every Norman to do a year's penance for each person they killed and if they weren't sure how many they had slain then to build a church instead.

There was also an economic boom in the late eleventh century and beyond, while castle building created jobs, and provided the focus of new trading centres. Many English towns expanded after 1066, exports of wool to Flanders increased, and trade to southern Europe went up, while new settlements, such as Newcastle, Hull, Boston and Portsmouth, were built.[18] But all of this might have happened anyway, as Europe was entering a renaissance that would continue until growth was somewhat slowed by famine and plague wiping out half the population in the fourteenth century.

CHAPTER ELEVEN

William's Children All Kill Each Other

I f it was any consolation to the English, William's life would get progressively worse as he fell out with pretty much everyone, including his own wife, brother and children. After he died his three surviving sons then fought each other until one was dead in a mysterious hunting accident and another locked away in prison for three decades, and his grandchildren would spend another twenty years in conflict. William and eldest son Robert Curthose ('Fat legs' or 'shorty-pants', a nickname that his father had invented) hated each other. At Christmas 1078 Robert had managed to personally wound his father, and not by saying 'I wish I was never born', but literally in battle. William's life was, funnily enough, saved by an English soldier in his army, Toki son of Wigot, who died in the process.[1]

Robert had inherited his mother's short stature and while she doted on him, father and son did not get along. The eldest son was nothing like his father, affable, generous to the point of recklessness, but also the sort of spoilt prince who were common in the medieval period. As one historian put it, he 'had perhaps the greatest faults of character; his life was self-indulgent and purposeless'.[2] The potbellied aristocrat surrounded himself with a 'swarm of obsequious sycophants' who flattered him, and his court was notoriously seedy and debauched, with jesters and prostitutes of both sexes. He had little to do except wait for his father to die, and when Robert asked for land from him, the old man jeered at him and Robert stormed off, saying he would have revenge.

The great conflict between father and son was triggered in 1077 over, of all things, a practical joke. Robert's younger brothers William and Henry came along to Robert's hall one day, where he was feasting with his cronies. The two were in the balcony above playing dice and larking around when they decided to throw a chamber pot filled with fetid water or urine on Robert and his party below, as a prank. (Normans didn't have particularly sophisticated humour). Robert felt his dignity was damaged, and that the king should have taken his side. In a tantrum the twenty-six-year-old started to besiege the castle of Rouen.

It culminated in the battle of 1078 in which, according to one story, father and son fought each other in full armor without knowing who the other was until Robert recognized him and let his father go. Alas this story sounds too good to be true, but we don't know much about the outcome because the page of the *Anglo-Saxon Chronicle* describing Robert's rebellion was cut away, presumably because it reflected badly on the king.

Furthermore, when the monarch found out that Queen Matilda had been talking to Robert and secretly sending her grown-up son money, he felt bitterly betrayed and their previously solid relationship never really recovered. William had Samson, Matilda's messenger, arrested and blinded as punishment, which can't have helped the marriage.

Eventually William even fell out with his brother Odo, who was arrested in 1082 for a totally bizarre reason. Odo had been distributing money to the people of Rome as bribes, and was trying to recruit knights from England to invade the papal city, which sounds like an unhinged plan. Recruiting knights without the king's permission was a treasonable offence in itself—overthrowing the pope in a military coup was definitely a no-no, even back then. Apparently Odo had got the idea when a soothsayer told him the next pontiff would be called Odo, which seems an unwise reason. William also heard he had been making enquiries about whether any bishop had been king of England before.

Odo would not have been a popular choice. While William's other half brother Robert of Mortain was described as 'dense and slow-witted', the bishop was famously grasping about money and brutal in his dealings with rebels, 'dreaded by Englishmen everywhere'. In 1075 Odo had led an army against Waltheof and Ralph the Breton then again in 1080 after locals in Durham had murdered a bishop. Now William had him thrown in jail and nursed a burning hatred towards a man he had helped make vastly wealthy.

The following year William's wife died and the last restraining influence was gone—luckily though he would not be around for much longer. Things had got harder for the ageing warrior because the new king of the Franks, Philip I, became increasingly assertive and was also alarmed that one of his vassals now had a whole kingdom.

The year 1087 was a terrible one for England. The *Anglo-Saxon Chronicle* described it as 'a very heavy and pestiferous year in this land' and 'such a disease came on men that very nearly every other man had the worst illness'. The book, which was never cheery at the best of times, lamented how 'many hundreds of men died wretched deaths through the famine'.

The king was more hated than ever, although he spent most of his time in France fighting. In late summer he arrived in the town of Mantes, in the disputed Vexin region, besieged it and set it on fire. William was fifty-nine and grossly overweight, so fat that there were widespread jokes doing the rounds about him being pregnant. This latest conflict began after Philip I had invaded the Vexin; William sent out messengers to demand it back, and Philip replied 'When is the fat man going to have his baby?' William had been bedridden with stomach complaints, probably caused by obesity, but when he heard about the joke he replied that after going to Mass following the birth 'I will offer a hundred thousand candles on his behalf.' In other words—burn down Paris.

William was probably a bit too old and fat to be doing this sort of thing by now. During the siege of Mantes his horse jumped awkwardly, by one account frightened by the flames, and his saddle ripped into William's stomach; it became infected and he spent five or six weeks in agony, but at least he died doing what he loved best—burning down cities and killing its inhabitants. The *Anglo-Saxon Chronicle* reported that William perished after destroying 'all the holy churches in the city' and added that 'two holy men who served God' burned to death as a result. They also described with barely concealed glee how William then died soon after, so that 'he who had been a powerful king and lord of many lands now held no more than seven feet of earth'. The tone was such that they may as well have added 'LOL!' at the end.

Even William felt regret for all the oppression and brutality he had dished out, and on his deathbed speculated on his legacy: 'I fell on the English of the northern counties like a raving lion, subjecting them to the calamity of a cruel famine and by so doing became the barbarous murderer of many thousands, young and old, of that fine race of people. I have persecuted its inhabitants beyond all reason. Whether noble or commons I have cruelly oppressed them; many I have unjustly disinherited.'[3] If only modern politicians could be so honest in their autobiographies.

By his side were his sons William Rufus and Henry Beauclerc. Robert Curthose had chosen to remain in Paris with the king of France, a final snub.[4] However, as William had made the leading nobles of Normandy swear an oath to Robert back in 1063 he could not disinherit him now, and so Robert became duke. As for England he concluded: 'Having therefore made my way to throne of that kingdom by so many crimes I dare not leave it to anyone but God alone.' William added, however, that he would be pleased if God allowed Rufus to take the English throne.

He asked for the release of all the prisoners in his care, except for Odo, of whom he said: 'I imprisoned not a bishop but a tyrant and if he goes free, without doubt he will disturb the whole kingdom and bring thousands to destruction.' William was eventually persuaded to let his devious brother go but he was, of course, totally right.

Wulfnoth, Harold's luckless youngest brother, was finally released, only to be immediately rearrested and imprisoned by Rufus in a jail in England.

As the conqueror parcelled out his realms to his sons and noblemen, all his nearby possessions were ransacked in a rather undignified scene: 'The servants—seeing that their master had disappeared—laid their hands on the weapons, the old and silver plate, the rich cloth and the royal furniture. The corpse of the king was left almost naked on the floor.'

The king's body was then taken to Abbey of St Etienne in Caen to be buried but a 'yokel' called Ascelin Fitzarthur said it was his land and refused to allow it to go ahead until he was paid off by Henry. Then at the funeral William's corpse was so obese that his pallbearers collapsed under the weight of his coffin, and the body fell onto the church floor, stinking out the place and causing everyone to flee.

It's hard to conclude anything other than that his reign had been a total disaster for England, although one English chronicler begrudgingly admitted that 'one must not forget the peace he brought to this land, so that all men of property might travel safely through the kingdom'. But then, in much of the north, there was no one left to do any crime.

William Rufus quickly hurried from Normandy to Westminster to claim the throne before Robert could murder him. Meanwhile

Henry, the youngest of William's nine or ten children by Matilda, received £5,000, a fortune but still rather small compared to a whole country. So much did he trust his father that Henry sat counting it in front of him until satisfied it was all there.

William II, nicknamed Rufus because of his red hair and alcohol-soaked red face, was compared to his father a decent man but also 'a rumbustous, devil-may-care soldier, without natural dignity or social graces, with no cultivated tastes and little show of conventional religious piety or morality—indeed, according to his critics, addicted to every kind of vice, particularly lust and especially sodomy.'[5]

It was said of the younger William that 'he was loathsome to almost all his people, and abominable to God'. That, however, was a priest's view, and the new king made the mistake of alienating the clergy, and because most history was written by monks, William became the subject of many allegations, among them that he indulged in devil worshipping and homosexuality. One clergyman described his horror at the goings-on at the new king's court: 'The model for young men was to rival women in delicacy of person, to mince their gait and to walk with loose gesture and half naked.' Churchmen complained that unlike the hard men who hung around his father, the court was now full of 'prostitutes and parasites'.

Rufus, who had different color eyes and a stammer (possibly a result of his shouting father), and like his brother Robert was no intellectual, was also criticized for wearing a beard and long hair, a new fashion among Anglo-Norman aristocrats copied from the English. A chronicler called Orderick wrote of him: 'He had no lawful wife. But he gave himself insatiably to obscene fornications and frequent adulteries. Soiled by his sins, he set a guilty example of shameful debauchery to his subjects.' Apparently Rufus also held Roman-style orgies, but considering his father had murdered thousands, perhaps history can forgive his son a few Freddy Mercury–style escapades.

His blasphemy and contempt for Church finances further infuriated the priests; the king would regularly shout religious obscenities, his favorite being 'God's face!' which, although rather tame by modern standards, upset the authorities. When a nobleman complained that the king was taking all the Church's cash, he simply replied: 'What is it to you?' And even when a monk told Rufus that he had foreseen his death in a dream, the king shrugged it off; being a monk, he said, 'of course, he dreams for money'.

Worst of all William II had garnered a reputation for trying to extort money from any source available, and his cronies did likewise. Most notorious of all was the bishop of Durham, Ranulf Flambard, whose nickname meant 'incendiary', so called because of his thinly-veiled attempts to scam as many people out of as much cash as was possible: 'he skinned the rich, ground down the poor, and swept other men's inheritances into his net'.[6] Another one of William's tactics was to give bishops long holidays so his favourites could use their properties while they were away; he also kept church positions empty so he could rake in the money they generated.

William Rufus was also addicted to food, and almost ate himself to death in 1093. He had made a promise to the Church when he thought he was dying about being a good Christian and doing whatever they said, but afterwards he went back on everything he had said.

After Archbishop Lanfranc had died in 1089 the king left the see vacant for four years but eventually invited Anselm, abbot of Bec in Normandy, to replace him. Anselm refused. The king begged, and then he ordered everyone in the chamber to prostrate themselves before the churchman. He refused still. The courtiers then pulled Anselm by his head, and gave him the staff, and when he refused they prised open his fingers—and they then cried out 'Long live the bishop'. He was carried to the nearest church for his installation, still protesting.

The relationship didn't last, however, and only four years later William had Anselm exiled. The two men had disagreed on a range of ecclesiastical issues, in the course of which the king declared of his archbishop that, 'Yesterday I hated him with great hatred, today I hate him with yet greater hatred and he can be certain that tomorrow and thereafter I shall hate him continually with ever fiercer and more bitter hatred. As for his prayers and benedictions, I spit them back in his face.'[7]

Just as his brother had predicted, within weeks Bishop Odo was conspiring to cause trouble, provoking a rebellion against Rufus with the backing of Robert, who also sought the crown of England. However this revolt was rather half-hearted, and only two major noblemen were involved, another Eustace of Boulogne and the villainous Robert of Bellême. Bellême, the grandson of the bishop who had strangled his wife and burned down his own cathedral, was notorious even for the standards of the day, described as 'Grasping and cruel, an implacable persecutor of the Church of God and the poor . . . unequalled for his iniquity in the whole Christian era.' He had his wife put in a dungeon, and as one historian described him: 'In a society of ruffianly, bloodthirsty men, Robert of Bellême stands out as particularly atrocious; an evil, treacherous man with an insatiable ambition and a love of cruelty for cruelty's sake; a medieval sadist whose ingenious barbarities were proverbial among the people of that time'.[8] He inspired the medieval folk story *Robert the Devil*, about a nobleman who discovers Satan is his father, which later became an opera. The conqueror had distrusted him so much he had garrisoned his castle, a highly unusual move.

Threatened with another invasion from Normandy, William II offered the English fairer laws if they fought with him against his brother. Promises which he had no intention of keeping. The *Chronicle* says 'he promised them the best law that ever was in this land; and forbade every unjust tax and gave me and their woods and their coursing—but it did not last long'.[9]

In fact when in 1094 Rufus proposed invading Normandy, and lots of English soldiers turned up with ten shillings for their provisions (raised by every taxpayer in the district), he took their money then sent them home,[10] like a proto-internet scam. When Lanfranc had once told off William for lying all the time he replied 'Who can be expected to keep all his promises?'

The country faced yet another fratricidal civil war, but luckily events far away came to the rescue. In 1095 Pope Urban II preached a crusade to win back the Holy Land for Christendom; it came about after the Byzantine emperor called for western Christian help following a series of defeats to the Seljuk Turks, although the Greeks would soon regret inviting the Latin Christians east.

Robert was among those who volunteered to go and fight, and to raise funds he loaned Normandy to his brother William, raising the money by extorting money from landlords and pillaging the Church. Various aristocrats went off, among them not just Robert but also Edgar Atheling, William's mild-mannered son-in-law Stephen of Blois, who was married to the famously strong willed and bossy Adela, and Eustace of Boulogne's sons Godfrey and Baldwin. Also along for the ride was that paragon of Christian virtue Odo, who died en route in Italy.

By January 1098 they were all starving outside of Antioch. Stephen of Blois wrote to his wife saying that it was a terrible place and that 'throughout this winter we have endured intense cold and incessant rain'. Stephen had enough of the whole thing and went back home, but his wife eventually forced him to return, wearing him down with 'these speeches and many more like them'.[11] This time he died, but by the sounds of things death might have been a release for Stephen.

Ghastly though it was, unlike subsequent crusades this one was at least successful, and in 1099 they captured Jerusalem and rather set the tone for the next few centuries by massacring all the Muslims and, for some reason, Jews. Along the way they had killed countless eastern Christians too, because they were either too stupid to understand the difference or didn't care. Eustace's son Godfrey of Boulogne became Defender of the Holy Sepulchre in 1099 and was succeeded by his brother Baldwin the following year, who took the title King of Jerusalem. Compared to this, 'king of England' seems like a pretty so-so job title.

With Jerusalem conquered, Robert was desperate to get back to avoid his brother taking over Normandy forever. As it happens William was having something of a hard time himself and things were going badly; well as bad as they could be, really. In August 1100 he was out hunting in the New Forest when one of his party, Walter Tirel, accidentally shot him, the king making it worse by trying to pull out the arrow shaft. Luckily his loyal brother Henry was nearby, and had the killer quietly sent to France and let off, while he quickly rushed to Winchester to claim the throne. Within three days Henry had himself crowned, having turned up with a heavily armed retinue and suggesting to the clergy they make him king.

What's also strange is that Tirel mistook Rufus for a deer when, even if the sun was in his eyes, he was supposed to be the best shot in the land; it was even stranger that Henry happened to be nearby with Tirel's brothers-in-law, who were both subsequently given gifts of land. There's always been a touch of suspicion about the way William II died in a mysterious hunting 'accident', but it was a dangerous sport and accidents without inverted commas were also quite frequent—the Conqueror's second son Richard was killed in the exact same forest around 1070, and there were no conspiracy theories at the time.[12] But if it was not an accident, then it was lucky for Henry, since Robert was still on his way back from the Holy Land. The eldest brother had been broke when he left but now he had not just the glory of winning back Jerusalem, but had also picked up a beautiful and rich wife on the way back.

The sacrilegious king was buried at Winchester Cathedral, which collapsed the following year. Most believed it was a sign from above, although William of Malmesbury simply pointed out that 'it was badly built'.

William was not a success, but he did leave one great legacy in Westminster Hall, which he built so he could fit in his new marble throne. When it was completed he had said: 'It is big enough to be one of my bedchambers'. It's still there, the oldest surviving part of the Palace of Westminster, and was where the Queen Mother was laid in state after she died in 2002.

CHAPTER TWELVE

Nineteen Long Winters When Christ and His Angels Slept

As one historian said of King Henry I, 'From the moral standpoint he was probably the worst king that has occupied the throne of England'.[1] Relentlessly greedy, cruel and sex mad, he was clever enough to keep the Church onside so he could concentrate on his main interests—sex and money. A thickset man with black hair, 'a steady gaze and an unfortunate tendency to snore', during his long reign Henry managed to sire between twenty-two and twenty-five illegitimate children by up to eight different mistresses, which is to date the English royal record.[2] Still, at least the Church couldn't accuse him of being gay. Although not husband of the year by any measure, Henry's chronicler/propagandist William of Malmesbury said of him that 'All his life he was completely free from fleshly lusts, indulging in the embraces of the female sex, as I have heard from those who know, from love of begetting children and not to gratify his passions'. I'm sure he hated every minute of it.

Soon after becoming king he had married Edith, the daughter of Malcolm III of Scotland and Edgar Atheling's sister Margaret, so giving Henry both peace with the Scots and a greater claim to rule the English.[3] He had to change his wife's name to Matilda because the Normans refused to accept anyone with an English name; however the Norman aristocracy thought Henry had gone native and mockingly referred to the royal couple as 'Godric and Godiva' and Henry as 'King of the English'. Born in Yorkshire and able to speak the native language, he was the only Norman king who was genuinely popular, partly at least because he made a sop to tradition, such as reestablishing county and local courts 'according to the laws of Edward' (the Confessor). But this was all for show, for 'he could flatter the English when he had need of their help, but he really detested them'.[4]

Like the Conqueror, he was notoriously greedy, and obsessed with the idea that someone might be ripping him off somewhere, and this led to the great innovation of his reign. King Henry wanted to make the kingdom more efficient, and so ordered that every sheriff bring him each county's revenues twice a year; here he would personally count out the money (a pound was the weight of 240 silver pennies, the currency of Anglo-Saxon times) on a large table with a chequered cloth, or exchequer, on top of it. As a result the new government treasury became known as the exchequer, and has remained so ever since; today the head of the British Treasury is called the Chancellor of the Exchequer. (Henry also founded the country's first zoo, near Woodstock in Oxfordshire.)

The king's greed chimed with his ruthless violent streak; after replacing all the coins in 1124, because of their poor quality, he ordered all the kingdom's coin producers to come to him where he condemned half of them to have their right hand and genitals cut off.[5] It was this no-nonsense approach to law and order that gave him his nickname the 'Lion of Justice', this sort of outright cruelty being popular with most of the population. The *Chronicle* says of

Henry I: 'In his time no man dared do wrong against another; he made peace for man and beast.'

Henry kept the bishops onside, but he was cynically pious; he made a grand gesture of promising to honor the Church, but like his brother he also kept bishoprics vacant so he could take in the money. His favorite oath was 'By God's death' but no one seemed to mind, because he didn't interfere with Church finances. Henry promoted Roger of Salisbury to archbishop because he said Mass the quickest, and tried to make his doctor archbishop of Canterbury, although the bishops blocked it as they thought it an inappropriate job for a man who inspected women's urine. The great lasting religious contribution of his reign came from one of his knights, Rahere, who was struck with malaria on a pilgrimage to Rome and promised to build a hospital in London if he recovered. He did, and St Barts in central London is today the capital's oldest hospital. As well as helping the sick, Rahere was also an enthusiastic jester, and would regularly juggle in front of amused inpatients as they arrived at the hospital.

Unlike his elder brothers Henry was educated to a high degree, his nickname, *beauclerc*, meaning 'fine scholar', and he once said that an illiterate king was little better than a crowned donkey. Education did not make him a better person, however, and in many ways he was the most sinister of all of William's family; in 1090 Henry was fighting Norman rebels with his brother Robert against William and dealt with one, Conan Pilatus, by throwing him out of a castle window, despite the man pleading for his life. During a hostage situation with a rebel knight and his own illegitimate daughter, he ordered two of his granddaughters to be blinded; their mother Juliana de Fontevrault tried to assassinate him afterwards, with a crossbow. And he once blinded a Norman minstrel who sang a song critical of him; in comparison his elder brother Robert was like a harmless upper-class buffoon.

Curthose returned from his religious duties in 1101 and prepared to invade England. He might have won, but foolishly agreed to negotiations. Under their agreement, Henry made him heir in England and gave him a pension on condition he go back across the channel; then in April 1105 Henry invaded Normandy where he burned down Bayeux Cathedral. The following year, on September 28, 1106—forty years to the day after the Normans arrived in England—an Anglo-Norman force under Henry defeated and captured Robert.

The Conqueror's eldest son was kept prisoner in Cardiff for twenty-eight years, living to the age of eighty, by which time he was so bored that he had learned Welsh, but he had left behind a son, William Clito. In 1119 Clito had joined forces with the French king Louis the Fat to drive Henry out. With customary ruthlessness Henry burned down another cathedral, at Evreux, to drive out the opposition, although this time he had got approval of its bishop and promised to rebuild it afterwards. Clito fought in direct conflict with his cousin, Henry's son William 'Adeling'; they were around the same age, seventeen and sixteen respectively, and both their names meant 'throne-worthy', one in Latin and the other in English. When they fought at Brémule in August 1119 Henry's side was victorious and Clito fled with Louis the Fat—who as his name suggests wasn't the greatest warrior in the world. The next day Henry returned Louis's warhorse with its trappings and Adeling sent back Clito's horse 'with a selection of rich gifts for his defeated cousin in an exquisitely judged gesture of chivalric condescension.'[6] A year later Louis recognized Henry and his son as rulers of Normandy, and after this triumph his followers gathered at the port of Barfleur in November in order to sail back to England. They were in celebratory mood.

The king's boat had sailed ahead, and William Adeling was behind on board the White Ship, the most state-of-the-art and luxurious vessel of the age, which was captained by the son of the very man who had brought the Conqueror over in 1066. Alongside him were two hundred other high-spirited young Normans, including Richard of Lincoln, Henry's favourite bastard, and another of the king's backstreet offspring, the Countess of Perche. Before setting sail some 'three casks of wine', a staggering 775 litres, had already been emptied by the passengers and crew[7]—four bottles per person. Henry's favourite nephew Stephen was on board but could not drink because of a stomach upset; alarmed by the state of the crew, he asked to be put ashore.

Being paralytically drunk, the seafarers naturally thought it a great idea to accept the revellers' dare to catch up with the king's ship ahead of them. The boat hit some rocks, and became one of several thousand to end up at the bottom of the channel, and most were killed below decks. The drowning youngsters were so close to land that their screams could be heard ashore, but were mistaken for hijinks, and they were left to die. William initially escaped in a lifeboat, only to go back to try to save his half sister—they were overwhelmed and all died.

After an hour only a butcher called Berold and a nobleman, Geoffrey Fitzgilbert, clung on to a raft and in the night the latter drifted to his death. Berold survived because of the rough sheepskin jacket 'so unlike the waterlogged silks and furs that had dragged the drowning courtiers down'; he was rescued by fishermen the next day.

In the morning, and with no sign of the boat, concern grew and then the worst fears were realized when bodies starting floating ashore. As news broke, the court fell into mourning—almost everyone had lost a loved one but it was many hours before a lowly pageboy was chosen to tell the king. Henry had to retire to a separate room, not wanting his subjects to see him cry, and for the remaining years of his life he was a broken man.

Afterwards Henry, mean as always, returned his son's widow Matilda of Anjou to her father Fulk but kept the dowry.

Henry died in 1135, supposedly by overdosing on lampreys, a type of eel that kills its prey by cutting its stomach and sucking out its insides; the fish was considered a delicacy at the time. Leaking black fluid, Henry's corpse was taken to Reading Abbey, which he had established as a memorial to his son. The king's embalmer was unskilled and died after inhaling the stench of the cadaver, 'the last of many whom King Henry had put to death', as Henry of Huntingdon said. After this William the Conqueror's grandchildren, true to family tradition, spent the next twenty years fighting each other, and as one monk wrote: 'Never did a country endure greater misery'.

The Anarchy

Such disasters were quite common in the Anglo-Norman kingdom, and in the mid-twelfth century more courtiers died from drowning than fighting for the crown.[8] But only this one would lead to civil war, a war appropriately known as 'the Shipwreck' or 'Anarchy'. Henry's only surviving child was yet another Matilda, who lacked the most important quality of medieval kingship, a penis. Neither the Franks, the English nor the Normans had ever had a female ruler, and they were not going to start now. However, when Henry made his nobles swear allegiance, there was a scrum to be first to pledge support for Matilda; after David, king of Scots, got there first, the king's illegitimate son Robert of Gloucester and nephew Stephen of Blois fought to be the second. Stephen won, but when the old king died most would go back on their oath.

Matilda had spent most of her life on the continent. At the age of just eleven she was betrothed to the German emperor Heinrich V, who was thirty-two, and she spent much of her second decade running Germany while her husband was away. Her time there was not exactly easy; at fourteen she was accompanying Heinrich on a war in Italy, crossing the hazardous Brenner Pass across the Alps. At this young age she already held the titles Queen of Germany and Queen of the Romans, and was popular, known to her German subjects as 'the good Matilda'.

However her husband died of cancer and now in her midtwenties Matilda headed back to England with only some mementoes of her time as Europe's most powerful woman, including two jewelled crowns of solid gold, 'one so heavy that it could only be worn when supported by two silver rods—and the mummified hand of the apostle St James'. She now found herself demoted, forced to marry the fifteen-year-old Geoffrey of Anjou, scion of a neighbouring county whose people the Normans viewed as vicious barbarians.[9] The marriage was not a success. In fact Matilda and Geoffrey were only married because of the threat posed by William Clito, who had become Count of Flanders, which made it necessary to acquire Anjou—and six weeks after their wedding Clito was stabbed to death in a fight with a foot soldier while preparing to attack his uncle yet again.

Within a year the couple were separated but Henry had forced them to get back together and soon two sons were born. Despite this the king still hated Geoffrey, partly because the Normans hated the Angevins, and partly because he just hated Geoffrey. So did the barons. In fact even Matilda hated Geoffrey, who came from a long and especially vicious line of murderers and sexual sadists. The king preferred his easygoing nephew Stephen, who he made the richest man in the kingdom through his largesse, and whom he had adopted virtually as a son.

Stephen was famously relaxed and unambitious and so it was a surprise that when Henry died he raced across the channel and arrived in Winchester, where his brother Henry was bishop, and had himself crowned. The most popular choice for king was Henry's son Robert of Gloucester, but he refused because he was illegitimate, an increasing sign of how strict European rulers were becoming about marriage. Stephen also had an older brother, but his name, William the Simple, rather explains why he was not in contention. He seems to have had a sort of personality disorder and after threatening to kill a priest was quietly encouraged to retire to a country house somewhere by their mother Adela, who instead pushed Stephen forward.

Nineteen years of war followed, a conflict that must have been of supreme indifference to the English peasantry; indeed there was only one proper battle, most of the conflict consisting of skirmishes, murder and general lawlessness. Kidnappings, robberies and killings rocketed, and local barons took the opportunity to lock people up and demand money from them, so that dungeons across the land were filled. This was 'feudal anarchy' in action, where local bigwigs with armed followers could do whatever they liked; atrocities during sieges were common, in order to grind down enemy morale, with corpses hanged from walls and prisoners taken by the attackers killed in clear view.

The *Anglo-Saxon Chronicle* entry of 1139 was especially depressing, describing how both sides in the civil war kidnap 'peasant men and women, and put them in prison for their gold and silver, and tortured them with unutterable torture . . . They hanged them by the thumbs, or by the head, and hung fires on their feet; they put knotted strings about their heads, and writhed [twisted] them so that it went to the brain . . . Some they put in a chest that was short, and narrow, and shallow, and put sharp stones therin, and pressed the man therein, so that they broke all his limbs . . . I neither can nor may tell all the wounds or all the tortures which they inflicted on wretched men in this land.'

The problem was that Stephen was too nice to be king. He had a very light voice, and had to get someone else to make speeches before battle. When Exeter rose in rebellion Stephen's brother Bishop Henry recommended massacring the rebels, pointing out that 'kingship rather than humanity' was the order of the day. On the other hand Robert of Gloucester suggested mercy, and so Stephen allowed the rebels to go free; Robert soon defected to his sister which suggested he might not have been giving Stephen the most helpful of advice.

Henry I or Canute would have hanged or blinded half the population on a good day, but Stephen was 'a mild, good-humoured, easygoing man, who never punished anybody', as the *Anglo-Saxon Chronicle* put it. In the eyes of most people this made Stephen weak.

Matilda was meanwhile hampered by her relatives. Soon after Stephen seized the throne the north was invaded by David of Scotland, Matilda's uncle, which probably wasn't a great help, since northerners were quite reasonably terrified of the Scots. Likewise her estranged juvenile husband Geoffrey, being an Angevin, was tremendously unpopular.

However in 1141 Empress Matilda was on the point of victory after Stephen had been taken captive outside Lincoln. He was led to Bristol in chains, but in September Matilda and her ally Robert of Gloucester were besieging Winchester when they were caught by an army loyal to Stephen. Robert heroically fought long enough to allow his sister to escape while he was captured. He was then exchanged for Stephen, and so they were back to square one.

We know less about the later stages, because its main chronicler, William of Malmesbury, unfortunately died in 1143; the last sentence of his last book, *Historia Novella*, reads 'I am disposed to go into this more thoroughly if ever by the gift of God I learn the truth from those who were present'.

Matilda meanwhile had sparked a riot in London, and such was her haste to escape the angry Londoners that she left her dinner unfinished, and for the rest of the conflict she spent her time running around the West Country. Londoners were angry partly because she'd taken away their town council but also that she could not protect them against an army sent by Stephen's ruthless wife, Eustace's daughter Matilda of Boulogne (often spelled Mathilde by historians just to make things a little bit easier). Mathilde led a harrowing of London with a 'magnificent body of troops . . . [who] raged most furiously around the city with plunder and arson, violence and the sword.' Londoners watched as 'their land was stripped before their eyes and reduced by the enemy's ravages to a habitation for the hedgehog'. Matilda now found that everyone who had previously supported her deserted, including Stephen's brother Bishop Henry, who two months earlier had proclaimed her Lady of England and 'cursed all who cursed her, blessed those who blessed her'. (St Bernard of Clairvaux called Bishop Henry 'the man who walks before Satan'.)

To make matters worse her husband Count Geoffrey, who was running Normandy as duke, now refused to help her by sending soldiers.

Matilda, who styled herself, 'Lady of the English', was also apparently haughty towards Londoners, although the hostile chroniclers who suggested this might have said this about any woman who ruled. One pro-Stephen account says: 'She at once put on an extremely arrogant demeanour instead of the modest gait and bearing proper to the gentle sex.'

Things only improved when the pope launched the Second Crusade in 1147, and many of the warring aristocrats went to fight there. The crusade itself was an absolute failure, and ended with the Christians all hating each other, but there were was one significant result; along the way the English contingent stopped in Lisbon, where the local Christians persuaded them to join an attack on the Saracens there, which they did, helping in the creation of Portugal.

With her support dwindling, Matilda fled from Oxford in 1149, escaping by rope from an open window and crossing the frozen river, she and her four companions camouflaged in white against the snow.

Eventually the war entered a new generation and was being fought by the eldest sons of the two claimants, Eustace and Henry Fitzempress. The Peterborough version of the *Chronicle* recorded of Stephen's son: 'He was an evil man and did more harm than good wherever he went; he spoiled the lands and laid thereon heavy taxes.' Matilda's son Henry, meanwhile, was something of a boy prodigy when it came to war. He had invaded England when he was aged just thirteen with some mercenaries but after a failed attempt to seize a castle his band of soldiers began to desert him and he was left stranded. Stephen, 'ever full of pity and compassion' bailed him out to send him home, like the parent of a spoiled gap year kid who's got in trouble with the police abroad.

Eventually the barons were so sick of the pointless conflict they began concluding private peace treaties. The earls of Leicester and Chester, whose land adjoined each other and were sworn to opposing sides, had a private deal that when they were called to have a war they would only turn up with twenty knights each and after the fight return all property that had been captured. In 1153 a peace was concluded but in a rage Eustace defied it by going on the rampage across East Anglia; he arrived at the Abbey of Bury St Edmunds, wrecked the lands when it refused his extortion demands, and then sat down for dinner in its refectory, where he choked to death.[10]

Tired of all the bloodshed, Stephen acknowledged Henry as his successor, and then died a year later of a stomach illness, perhaps the same condition that had saved his life twenty years earlier. Matilda lived for another fourteen years, acting as the king's advisor, her last piece of advice being for him to not hire his friend Thomas Becket as archbishop; like Harold, he should have listened to his mother.

The very last entry in the *Anglo-Saxon Chronicle* signed off in typically miserable style that same year: 'Never did a country endure more misery. If the ground was tilled the earth bore no corn, for the land was ruined by such doings; and men said openly that Christ and his saints slept.'

CHAPTER THIRTEEN

We Shall Never Surrender

An English farm in 1114 listed its workers as being called Soen, Rainald, Ailwin, Lemar, Godwin, Ordric, Alric, Saroi, Ulviet and Ulfac, while the manor was leased by a man called Orm.[1] Around the same time a boy from Whitby petitioned to change his name from Tostig to William because he was being bullied.[2] By the end of the century all these names had disappeared, and among the only surviving English monikers were Alfred, Edmund and in particular Edward, which remained in fashion because of the cult attached to Edward the Confessor. Henry III, Henry I's great-great-grandson, in the thirteenth century was so devoted that he named his first son Edward, starting a long line of kings by that name.

For a while a man's social class could immediately be deciphered just by his first name, and it is with enduring English class divisions that the Normans have always been associated. Certainly later, middle-class protestors against the aristocracy would see themselves as Saxons fighting against the Norman yoke, even if it was a bit of a fantasy.

Many on the parliamentary side during the English Civil War of 1642–49 saw their struggle as being the restoration of Saxon liberties taken away by a foreign tyrant, as they fought a Scottish-born monarch who was married to a French Catholic. The leader of the Diggers, Gerrard Winstanley, saw his band of Civil War radicals as inheritors of the Saxons against the Normans. In his crackpot pamphlet *The New Law of Righteousness*, which advocated a sort of Christian Communism, he argued that the Bible said everyone should be equal and: 'Seeing the common people of England by joynt consent of person and purse have caste out Charles our Norman oppressour, wee have by this victory recovered ourselves from under his Norman yoake.' This wasn't remotely true; before 1066 there was widespread slavery and vast inequality, but what differed after the conquest was that the oppressors spoke a different language. Winstanley, meanwhile, spent his last few years fighting over a small financial legacy he believed to be his.

Later, American revolutionaries such as Thomas Jefferson would identify with the defeated of 1066, seeing themselves as descendents and political successors of Harold's men. Jefferson, a keen student of Anglo-Saxon history, proposed that one side of the seal of the United States feature Hengest and Horsa, the semi-mythical fifth-century Jutish leaders who conquered Kent. And Thomas Paine warned that Americans under the British would find 'ourselves suffering like the wretched Britains under the oppression of the Conqueror'.

Much of this was more down to early modern attitudes to the French than anything. By the time of Jefferson France had long become the cultural leader of Europe, the center of sophisticated courtly manners and other aspects of high culture; but it was also run by a despotic aristocracy who treated their peasants appallingly and it was easy to transfer these qualities to the Normans.

In the nineteenth century Tory Prime Minister Benjamin Disraeli's idea that the country was divided by 'two nations' originated, he said, with 'the conquerors and the conquered'. In that same period one of Britain's most popular novels, Walter Scott's *Ivanhoe*, told the story of a heroic Saxon being hounded by the country's

Norman rulers while brave King Richard is off on crusade. The Victorian era, a high water mark for English national self-confidence and pro-German feeling, also saw peak Anglo-Saxonism. It was during this time that the Robin Hood myth, originally set in the 1260s and about economic discontent, was transferred to the 1190s and featured a Saxon rebel bandit resisting a Norman elite.

The idea has stuck, so that in his 1999 book on life as an activist for the British Labor Party, *Things Can Only Get Better*, John O'Farrell wrote: 'It struck me that the classes in Britain were still basically divided along the lines of Normans and Saxons. The Normans of Fulham still drank wine and owned land in France and the Saxons of Fulham still drank ale, used "Anglo-Saxon" vocabulary and tended small strips of land behind the playing fields.'[3] Britain at the time was led by a Tory with that most Anglo-Saxon of surnames, Thatcher.

Perhaps the Duke of Westminster's advice remains solid; research published in 2011 found that people with Norman surnames are still richer than the population as a whole, by some 10 percent on average.[4] However while most of the Anglo-Saxon elite fell at Hastings and large numbers were dispossessed, for many life went on as before, and a number of Anglo-Saxon gentry families did survive in their place. Among the thirteenth century 'landed' families who traced their line back to before 1066 were the Berkeleys, Cromwells, Nevilles, Lumleys, Greystokes and Audleys.[5]

The England that emerged from the Norman period was still recognizable as the Englalond of 1000, including its laws and culture. Matilda's son Henry II, a descendant of Edmund Ironside, would introduce the jury system that had its origins in Ethelred's reign. The Anglo-Saxon Witans would not be forgotten and remained potent symbols of nationhood; they were quoted during the debates over the Pennsylvanian constitution in 1776.

A number of Englishmen fled rather than accept Norman rule; some went to Scotland, where they tipped the linguistic balance

against Gaelic and ensured that country would be English speaking. Many others, perhaps enough to fill three hundred ships,
sailed to Constantinople to join the Emperor's Varangian guard.
The English Varangians even got to fight the Normans in Sicily,
and while it would be nice to say that here they got revenge alas
once again the Normans won; they generally tended to. Even more
bizarrely, some English refugees settled on the coast of the Black
Sea at a place, perhaps Crimea, that they called Nova Anglia, or
New England; this colony survived until the thirteenth century
when it was absorbed.[6]

The Normans did not stop in England, and would eventually
conquer Wales and Ireland. In 1098 the Norman Earls of Chester
and Shrewsbury were marching through North Wales in pursuit of
the local leaders Cadwgan and Gruffydd and were on the point of
capturing them when they met with sudden disaster in the form of
Magnus Barefoot, king of the Norwegians, who happened to be on a
sort of piracy holiday around the Irish Sea. The Earl of Shrewsbury
was among the Normans killed while the others fled. Alongside
Magnus was Harold Haroldson, son of the former king, who after
failing to start an uprising had eventually gone to Norway where
Magnus II treated him well because Harold had spared his life after
Stamford Bridge. After his trip with Barefoot, Magnus II's son, we
hear no more of him.

Meanwhile Harold's daughter Gunhild had became a nun at
Wilton in southern England where she was cured of a tumor by
Bishop Wulfstan of Worcester (the one who hated long hair). While
she was there the Breton Lord Alan the Red was supposed to be
married off to another nun, Edgar Atheling's niece Edith, but Alan
preferred Gunhild and abducted her. On top of this rather nonpro-
gressive form of wooing Alan had been at Hastings, and his brother
Brien had fought her brothers in Devon afterwards, but the two
seemed to have been happy together despite this obvious bone of
marital contention. After his death Gunhild married Alan's nephew,

another Alan. Meanwhile Edith's father Malcolm had tried to get William Rufus to marry his daughter instead but he wasn't the marrying type and she instead was matched to his brother Henry I.

Another of Harold's daughters, Gytha, fled to Denmark and was married to the far-flung Duke of Kiev. Their descendant Isabella of France would marry the ineffectual English king Edward II and through her the royal family, as well as the vast majority of English people,[7] can trace their descent to Harold as well as William.

The biggest impact of the Norman invasion was on the English language, which was replaced by French and Latin as the medium of government and law for three centuries. It might well have gone extinct, just as at least eight previous native languages of England had been, but most likely sheer weight of numbers and its established literature helped it survive.

Eventually English was adopted by the new aristocracy, but it was a changed language, and Old English is totally incomprehensible to us. Today at least a quarter and as many as a half of English words are of French origin, and the Norman invasion helped to add great nuance to the language. French words are usually more formal or aristocratic sounding: ascend, rather than rise, status rather than standing, mansion rather than house, cordial rather than hearty. Almost all words relating to government and justice are Norman, including *prison, jury, felony, traitor, govern* and, of course, *justice*. Likewise titles are mostly Norman French, including *sovereign, prince, duke* and *baron*—although not king or lord.

The most famous contrast is between the words for beasts in the field and those on plates, since the English words for animals—*pigge, sceap, cu*—survived, while the French terms for the dishes—*porce, mutton, boeuf*—took over. Words for semi-skilled trades like baker and shoemaker are Anglo-Saxon, while highly skilled, well-paid professions like mason and tailor are French. French-derived English words sound more flouncy, which is why George Orwell famously advised people to use Anglo-Saxon terms if possible.

Thanks to the Normans we have two words for many conditions, such as friendship and amity, brotherhood and fraternity, motherhood and maternity, rise and ascend, cheer and cherish, cave and cavern, stand and stay, cow and beef, think and pensive, smell and odour, help and aid, weep and cry, weird and strange, harbour and port, worthy and valuable, and knowledge and science.

Often the nouns stayed native while the adjective went French, so that we have water/aquatic, mouth/oral, son/filial and sun/solar. Another curious result was that in legal English this bilingualism led to lots of lexicon doublets, made up of an English and French word, such as breaking and entering, fit and proper, and wrack and ruin.

Curiously, some words have come to English both through Norman and Parisian French, giving us almost-twin doublets such as convey and convoy, gaol and jail, warden and guardian, warrant and guarantee, and wile and guile.[8]

Old English disappears as a written language soon after 1135, when the second to last *Anglo-Saxon Chronicle* was written just as the country slid into anarchy. Nineteen years later the last ever entry shows a language that was radically different, far closer to modern English than what went before. Anglo-Saxon used German constructions, with verbs at the end of the sentence, like Yoda from *Star Wars*. That all changed with the Normans. Gender was now on its way out, spelling was simplified, most of the conjugations were gone, and nouns were reduced to two inflections. If it wasn't for the Normans we'd all be speaking German; instead we speak a sort of pidgin German.

The very last piece of writing considered Old English dates from around 1190 in Canterbury; forty years later it is recorded that a monk at Worcester was trying to learn Old English but by 1300 some Anglo-Saxon text was noted as being an 'unknown language'; Middle English, the language of Geoffrey Chaucer, was born.

But it is not true that the Normans alone made English more French and less German. French may have become very influential anyway, as by the twelfth century it had become the *lingua franca* of western Europe, France the cultural centre of the continent for the next few hundred years, and most French words entered English after 1200, when the Normans were no longer in charge. In fact even before the conquest English had absorbed a number of French words, such as *bacon, ginger, capon, dancer, weapon, prison, service, market* and *proud*.[9] The period of peak borrowing was the last quarter of the fourteenth century, when 2,500 new loan words are identified; by this stage English had already replaced French as the language of Parliament, and England now occupied much of France rather than the other way around.[10] In contrast, in Layamon's *Brut* from around 1200, a popular verse history of the country, there are only 250 French loan words in thirty thousand lines, so the French influence must have come later.[11]

English would eventually replace Norman French as the language of government; in 1362 Parliament made English its official language while in 1399 Henry IV became the first king to have English as his native language since his ancestor Harold II. He opened Parliament by shouting 'Yes, yes, yes!' while his son Henry V would spend his short, spectacular career on a rampage through Normandy, as demented in his confidence in God's support as William I. Henry V, the prototype English soccer hooligan abroad, could barely understand French at all.

By 1385 English had recovered so well that someone wrote that 'nowadays children at grammar school know no more French than their left heel, and that is a misfortune for them if they should cross the sea and travel in foreign countries.' And things have barely changed since. It wasn't until the following century that English replaced French in courts, however, and a sort of 'degenerate French' was still used in law courts until the seventeenth century.[12]

Stephen's death in 1154 marked the end of the Norman age and the start of a new dynasty, called the Angevins or Plantagenets, after the type of flower Geoffrey of Anjou wore on his lapel in order to disguise himself while hunting. His son Henry II now ruled a vast empire that included the whole western half of France. This all came to an end when his incompetent son John lost Normandy in 1204, and from this point on the Anglo-Norman aristocrats began to see themselves as firmly English. While a judge in 1157 could speak of 'us Normans' needing protection 'against the wiles of the English'[13] just twenty years later crown treasurer Richard fitz Nigel observed 'the races have become so fused that it can scarcely be discerned who is English and who is Norman'. By that decade everyone could speak English fluently, and under John the reference to all subjects, 'Angli et Franci', was finally dropped from royal charters.

A disastrous attempt by John to win back his French lands in 1214 led to a revolt by the barons, which culminated the following year with a peace agreement called the 'great charter', or Magna Carta. The Anglo-Norman elite, many of whom were from mixed marriages, had become English, and their variation of French, cut off by the English Channel, was now laughed at in Paris. Today Norman, or 'Jersey French', remains one of three official languages in the Channel Islands, although almost no one can understand it. The islands were the only parts of the Duchy that remained in English hands after 1204 and today the Queen is still officially Duke of Normandy (not, strangely, duchess—the Normans would never accept a woman in charge, of course).

Driven underground, the English language could have gone altogether. Today only 4,500 of 30,000 Anglo-Saxon words are still in use in English, but not only did bits of Anglo-Saxon survive— it became the backbone of modern English. *In* fact *it is* impossible *to make any sense without it.* Today almost all of the most common hundred English words predate the conquest; the most popular French-derived word is *just*, ranked at 105.

Famously, when in 1940 Britain faced an invasion more devastating than that of 1066 its war time leader Winston Churchill made a speech that King Harold might have understood: 'We shall fight on the beaches; we shall fight on the landing grounds; we shall fight in the fields and the streets; we shall fight in the hills; we shall never surrender.' All but the final word are of Anglo-Saxon origin.[13]

Almost nine centuries after the conquest an enormous armada was launched in the opposite direction, comprised of the armies of three English-speaking nations, Britain, the United States and Canada. The British forces in the 1944 invasion of Normandy were led by Field Marshal Bernard Montgomery, from a Norman family that had settled in Scotland in the twelfth century. His ancestor Roger de Mundegumbrie had made the reverse trip with William. Bayeux was captured by the British on June 7, 1944, and at the graveyard of the 56th British infantry division which took the town, less than a mile from where the tapestry can now be viewed, there is today a Latin inscription which reads: *Nos a Guillelmo victi, victoris patriam liberavimus*: 'Those whom William conquered returned to liberate the land of the conqueror.'

Bibliography

This is an introduction to the subject and far more can be discovered in detail from the following:

Ackroyd, Peter *Foundations*
Asbridge, Thomas *The Greatest Knight*
Bartlett, Robert *The Making of Europe*
Barlow, Frank *The Godwins*
Borman, Tracy *Matilda. Queen of the Conqueror*
Bradbury, Jim *The Battle of Hastings*
Bridge, Anthony *The Crusades*
Bridgeford, Andrew *1066: The Hidden History of the Bayeux Tapestry*
Brooke, Christopher *The Saxon and Norman Kings*
Bryson, Bill *Mother Tongue*
Castor, Helen *She-Wolves*
Clarke, Stephen *1000 years of Annoying the French*
Crossley-Holland, Kevin *The Anglo-Saxon World*
Clements, Jonathan *Vikings*
Crystal, David *The Stories of English*
Denzinger, Danny and Lacey, Robert *The Year 1000*
Gimson, Andrew *Gimson's Kings and Queens*
Higham, Nicholas J. and Ryan, Martin J. *The Anglo-Saxon World*
Hindley, Geoffrey *The Anglo-Saxons*
Howarth, David *The Year of the Conquest*
Lacey, Robert *Great Tales of English History*

McLynn, Frank *1066*
Morris, Marc *The Norman Conquest*
Neveux, Francois *A Brief History of the Normans*
Oliver, Neil *The Vikings*
O'Brien, Harriet *Queen Emma and the Vikings*
Ormrod, W. H. *The Kings and Queens of England*
Parker, Philip *The Norseman's Fury*
Poole, A.L. *Domesday Book to Magna Carta*
Ramirez, Janina *The Private Lives of the Saints*
Schama, Simon *A History of Britain, Volume 1*
Stanton, Sir Frank *The Anglo-Saxons*
Strong, Roy *The Story of Britain*
Tombs, Robert *The English and Their History*
White, R.J. *England, A History*
Wood, Harriet Harvey *The Fall of Anglo-Saxon England*

Endnotes

Introduction

1. http://www.etymonline.com/index.php?term=bigot.
2. Malfoy translates as 'bad faith' and Voldemort as 'theft of death'. Without laboring the point almost all the Harry Potter villains have French-sounding aristocratic names, including Professor Quirinus Quirrell and Bellatrix Lestrange. In contrast goodies Dumbledore, Hagrid and Black all sound Anglo-Saxon. Granger, being the Anglo-Norman word for bailiff, is the exception to my half-baked theory.
3. https://www.ft.com/content/57f2dec2-5e7d-11e6-bb77-a121aa8abd95.
4. As a young man the duke had joined the army, as befitting someone of his class, although his passion was for the working-class sport of soccer. His father prevented him from signing for Fulham Football Club because he thought the sport involved too much unmanly kissing and he preferred upper-class rugby.
5. The concept is highly disputed among historians anyway. Some believe the definition is basically meaningless.

Chapter 1

1. See *Saxons vs Vikings*, book 2 in the series, for further information. More importantly, buy it.
2. Tombs, Robert.

3. Tombs.
4. Tombs.
5. The historian Robert Tombs argues that French literature only began in England after 1066 in imitation of English, and that the French epic *The Song of Roland*, about a heroic but rather dim-witted attack on the Saracens by the Franks, was written in England. In fact in real life Roland fought fellow Christians, not Saracens, but like Hollywood producers epic poets were casual about historic accuracy.
6. The English were new to all this, and one chronicler in Italy wrote that the English traders in Pavia once started an enormous brawl over excise duty.
7. The book states that all the children agree that they should make peace with the farmer 'because he provides us with food and drink . . . No matter who or what you are, whether a priest, or a monk, or a peasant, or a soldier, concern yourself with the task before you and perform it, and be what you are, for it is very harmful and disgraceful for a man not to know who and what he is and what he needs to be.'
8. The *Colloquy* includes a proud hunter, employed by the king, who catches stags in nets and hunts boards with lances, and says 'A hunter can't afford to be timid, because all kinds of wild animals live in the woods'. The Fisherman says he takes from lakes and rivers 'eels and pike, minnows, trout . . . and whatever small fish happen to be swimming in the river'.
9. Father's Day was only invented in West Virginia in 1908 in dedication to 361 miners who died in an explosion the previous December.
10. Among the other surviving works of the era is *The Twelve Charms*, which dates from the tenth and eleventh centuries, and includes a chant to pray for good crops with the magic words '*Erce, Erce, Erce, eorpan motor*'. *Eorpan motor* means 'mother of earth' and '*Erce*' supposedly refers to a long-forgotten fertility goddess, although it could just be nonsense.

11. Slavery also brought some revenue in for the crown: when a horse was sold buyer and seller would each pay a penny, when a man was sold they paid four pence.
12. From the Old English for 'to move', as in the German *fahren*. Much of Old English resembles German.
13. Howarth, David.
14. Stanton, Sir Frank.

Chapter 2

1. Ramirez, Janina.
2. Hilda Roderick Ellis Davidson, *Gods and Myths of Northern Europe*.
3. Almost all of England's counties existed by this point, except two in the far north and Rutland, a tiny area which historically was the dowry given to the Queen of England.
4. Or at least Byrhferth's *Life of St Oswald* says so.
5. She's more accurately called Ælfthryth but all the names of this period can be spelt a number of ways and I've tried to make them as simple as possible to avoid you feeling like you're trying to follow a baffling foreign novel.
6. O'Brien, Harriet.
7. Dunstan also apparently let rip at Ethelred's baptism, according to twelfth century historian William of Malmesbury, shouting 'By God and His Mother, he will be a wastrel when he is a man'. That sounds like the sort of thing you remember yourself saying much later.
8. The Vikings never touched what is now US soil, however, and the Nordic inscription discovered in Minnesota in 1898, the Kensington Runestone, is generally regarded as a hoax. But they did get as far south as Newfoundland, which is impressive enough.
9. The Normans were called 'The gray foreigners' on account of their chainmail. Vikings were also called 'the blue men'.
10. http://www.irishtimes.com/news/why-people-in-iceland-look-just-like-us-1.1104676.

11. The more poetic story is that two of the Rus visited the majestic Hagia Sofia in Constantinople and felt that they were close to heaven, and although it is a truly magnificent building the more likely explanation is that, as Vladimir himself said, 'Drinking is the joy of all Rus. We cannot exist without that pleasure.' One can imagine that the Islamic pitch to the Rus must have stumbled when this small print was mentioned. 'Hang on, have those other guys left?'

12. Ibn Fadlan's story became the basis for the Michael Crichton novel, *Eaters of the Dead*, later turned into the film, *The 13th Warrior*.

13. Clements, Jonathan.

14. "The Fortunes of Men" trans. Henry Morley. *The Library of the World's Best Literature. An Anthology in Thirty Volumes.* 1917, http://www.bartleby.com/library/poem/264.html.

15. *The Phoenix* is a happier poem, about the time of the 'happy Land' where the Phoenix live, where 'neither warm weather nor winter sleet can work the least harm here'. Then there is *Waldere*, a poem about Walter of Aquitaine, a Visigoth king on the run from Attila the Hun who fights another prince, Guthere, to impress his lover; again, though, only fragments remain. This story ends happily, but generally speaking the poetry at the time was bleak.

16. *Anglo-Saxon Riddles of the Exeter Book*, trans. PAULL F. BAUM. Durham, North Carolina: Duke University Press, 1963.

17. Ibid.

Chapter 3

1. Continental Saxons from what is now Germany, not to be confused with the Saxons who teamed up with the Angles in Britain.

2. Ragnar, whose surname means hairy trousers, appears in various sagas, dying a number of times and becoming father to an improbable number of Viking leaders. Today he is probably most famous as the lead character in the TV series *Vikings*.

3. http://www.ibtimes.co.uk/did-normans-descend-vikings-what-genetics-tell-us-about-viking-legacy-1560298.

4. Bradbury, Jim.

5. This became a place of devotion after St Michael the Archangel had appeared to a local bishop and, he claims, punched him in the head, which seems strikingly aggressive for a visitation, but then the Normans were violent people and maybe that was the only way the angel could get his attention. The bishop's head is still on display and does indeed contain a skull fracture.

6. O'Brien.

7. According to William of Malmesbury, the most important English historian of the period.

8. William of Jumieges, who was writing not long after the events, said that Ethelred defiled the kingdom 'with such a dreadful crime that in his own reign even the heathens judged it is a detestable, shocking deed.' Murdering 'the Danes who lived peacefully and quite harmoniously throughout the kingdom . . . he ordered the women to be buried up to the waists and the nipples to be torn from their breast by ferocious mastiffs set upon them. He also gave orders to crunch little children against doorposts'. William was a propagandist for the Normans, though, so he was probably lying.

9. Harald achieved a more lasting fame when Scandinavian cell phone engineers came up with a new device that would be able to make cross border communication easier, and decided to name it after a king who had united Norway and Denmark.

10. O'Brien.

11. In Bernard Cornwell's *The Last Kingdom* the protagonist, the Northumbrian Uhtred, is supposed to be an ancestor of the real Uhtred.

12. He didn't made a huge impact on the country, and as king of England Sweyn's only act was levying a tax in the area under his control which was returned after he died.

13. His name in Danish was Cnut, literally 'knot', but this sounds too pretentious and rude in English. In fact his real baptismal name was Lambert.
14. This is one theory at least. Many dispute it.
15. While Bishop of London Wulfstan once warned: 'Woe then to him who has earned for himself the torments of Hell. There there is everlasting fire roiling painfully, and there there is everlasting filth. There there is groaning and moaning and always constant wailing. There there is every kind of misery, and the press of every kind of devil. Woe to him who dwells in torment: better it were for him that he were never born, than that he become thus.'

Chapter 4

1. Although it sort of survives in the name of the Wizengamot, the council of wizards led by Dumbledore in the Harry Potter books.
2. Queen Emma's autobiography merely says 'God intervened' and took away Edmund, who was to be the last fully English king for some time.
3. Curiously Edmund is the subject of a play believed by some to have been Shakespeare's first, *Edmond Ironside (The English King)* although most experts now ruefully accept it wasn't.
4. There is still a St Clement Danes in the City of London, which features in the nursery rhyme *Orange and Lemons.*
5. East Anglia went to Thorkell the Tall, Mercia went to Eadric and Northumbria to his old friend Eric. Canute kept Wessex, the most important part and from where any native resistance was likely to come from.
6. Oliver, Neil.
7. A lot of historians don't like the term but it's useful and the quality and quantity of historical record hugely increases from the eleventh and twelfth centuries.

8. The relationship between church and state was also established after the Holy Roman Emperor and the pope met at an alpine pass and formally settled on the division and later this would be important in developing into the idea of secularism, that is that the church does not set secular laws and vice versa.

9. Most rules vastly exaggerated the extent of their power in their titles, with King Edgar calling himself 'Autocrat of All Albion and its Environs'. However in Rome Canute with typical Scandinavian modesty describes himself as 'King of all England and Denmark and the Norwegians and of some of the Swedes'. Not of all Sweden, just some of them.

Chapter 5

1. Barlow, Frank.

2. The 'warming pan myth', that the baby was snuck in during a fake 'birth' in a warming pan, is a recurring historical theme, most famously used against the son of the Catholic James II, whose birth in 1688 triggered a revolt by Protestant lords. A modern version is the legend that Barack Obama was actually born in Kenya and therefore an illegitimate ruler.

3. One theory at any rate. From Godwins.

4. Barlow.

5. Sweyn died soon after arriving in Denmark but on the plus side got a small cameo role in *Macbeth*.

6 Although some historians say she may have just been 'symbolically' naked, without jewellery. If this was the case, it was either a mistranslation, or the most wildly exaggerated story in history.

7. The procession fell into decline in the midnineteenth century because sexually repressed Victorians were fighting to get to the front to see the specially chosen local woman in tight clothes, and killjoys turned against it. It sadly disappeared in the twentieth century, although there have been attempts to revive it.

Chapter 6

1. Samuel Johnson, who created the first dictionary in the eighteenth century, received it from Queen Anne as a boy.
2. McLynn, Frank.
3. Sources are divided about whether it was consensual or rape. Also about whether she was actually related. At any rate it horrified everyone.
4. This ancient custom was called 'carrying the wolf's head' in Anglo-Saxon England; in other words the person could be hunted down like a wolf.
5. Barlow.
6. In 1066 Ralph's son Harold was too young to be a threat and was still around during the *Domesday Book*, listed as a landowner in the Midlands.
7. Many of the Normans then went up to Scotland, where King Mac Bethad mac Findlaich used them to cause trouble on the English border.
8. It was Eustace's men who accompanied Prince Alfred during his ill-fated trip to England and he may have feared a similar ambush, thus the hostile approach which proved self-fulfilling.
9. The *Chronicle* only refer in passing to 'the old lady' dying, which must have pleased her no end.
10. Barlow.
11. McLynn.
12. For example, it is still the law in some border towns to kill any Welshman after dark, largely because the medieval laws have never been officially repealed, but they have been superseded by other laws, and legal experts are *fairly* confident you wouldn't get away with it today.
13. The northern part of Northumbria, in the modern counties of Durham and Northumberland, remained more English and was still controlled by the old ruling house of Northumbria.

14. Perhaps Tostig was put in charge of the army, Harold of the treasury, and this lead to their rivalry.

Chapter 7

1. However the Europeans did change the pieces: the queen was originally a vizier, a sort of prime minister, while the bishop used to be an elephant.
2. Quoted in Bartlett, Robert, *The Making of Europe*.
3. Bartlett.
4. Tombs.
5. Howarth.
6. Robert tried to persuade the girl's father to let him sleep with her without any promise of marriage and without her permission, but was rebuffed. However he charmed her and they had a night of passion.
7. Although some historians doubt it. According to Howarth, Herleve's father Fulbert was perhaps a burgess, that is a city person of some status, and her brothers appear on charters, which suggest they were fairly high ranking.
8. McLynn.
9. Another story has William and Matilda having a domestic row at which point he dragged her through Caen by her hair, and this display of manliness impressed her so much she agreed he was right.
10. It's a testimony to the importance of Norman women that the number of daughters a couple had was only vaguely recorded. William and Matilda had five or six; he may have had daughters called Agatha and Adeliza or this may have been the same person. The chroniclers may as well have just written 'some daughters or whatever'.
11. On the other hand some historians say it's a myth and she was actually five feet tall, which was only a couple of inches below the average.

12. Borman, Tracy.

13. It's probably not true that local lords also claimed the right to sleep with their peasants' wives—the *droit de seigneur*—as this was only referenced in the sixteenth and seventeenth centuries, when people often made up or exaggerated how ghastly the medieval period was. It was in fact then that the term 'medieval' was invented as an insult. There's no need to exaggerate how awful the medieval world was—for most people it was horrific enough.

14. In one incident in 1014 a knight is recorded as taking it off to avoid detection after a battle was lost.

15. Quoted in *The Battle of Hastings*, Bradbury, Jim.

16. Only three of these are definite murders; two of them were strangled and one starved to death. Of the other four, two were allegedly poisoned, one strangled and one smothered.

17. William of Malmesbury.

18. At the council held to investigate the Norman bishops Ivo was asked 'What did you do, you perfidious man? you should be condemned by the law for daring to consign your mother to the flames'.

19. This is a fairly dubious story, to be fair. But Harold is certainly known to have had a sense of humour.

Chapter 8

1. Schama, Simon.

2. McLynn.

3. Bradbury.

4. The town had been founded in 965 by Norseman Thorgls 'Skarthi', the hairlipped, and is probably most famous for the fair that inspired the song of the name. The lyrics date back to the nineteenth century but it may be medieval in origin.

5. Howarth.

6. A recent example is the television series *Vikings*.

7. http://aclerkofoxford.blogspot.co.uk/2014/09/the-battle-of-stamford-bridge.html.

8. This is the higher of the two estimates by historians of the time, the other being five hundred. The human tendency to exaggerate being what it is, it's always safer to go for the lower figure.

Chapter 9

1. Morris, Marc.
2. A pinch of salt should be added here: stories about invaders falling and landing on the shore are quite perennial. The same thing was said about Julius Caesar and later Edward III in the 100 Years War.
3. It's believed that the route of the Norman army can be traced from the 1086 *Domesday Book* and the parts of Sussex listed as 'wasta', or empty land.
4. William of Malmesbury.
5. Or perhaps it was ten or eleven a.m. Only three actual accounts of the battle exist.
6. At the time it was reported as his 'leg', although the knight in question certainly wouldn't have been punished for such an attack.
7. William Malet is the only Norman whose successors today can definitely trace their descent in the male line directly to someone who actually fought at Hastings. This used to be a prestigious thing to claim in England, and there were often bitter arguments about pedigree.
8. https://familysearch.org/wiki/en/England_Pre-Norman_Conquest _Surnames_(National_Institute)
9. A church in Sussex, where Canute's daughter is believed to be buried, may also hold his remains, although the Church of England has to date refused to allow an exhumation, which are only carried out in exceptional circumstances.
10. Battle Abbey was only bought by the British government in 1976 with funds raised by American citizens, Britain being a basket case at the time; something perhaps worth mentioning when you're asked for the entrance fee.
11. Bridgeford, Andrew.

12. Bridgeford.
13. In a similar way the owners of Stonehenge used to hire out small axes so that visitors could chip bits off as mementos.

Chapter 10

1. Stanton.
2. Tombs, Robert.
3. Tombs.
4. *Surrey Folk Tales* by Janet Dowling.
5. The word wasn't coined until 1776, first appearing in Adam Smith's capitalist bible *The Wealth of Nations*.
6. Having said that, if you wanted to hunt well you needed a fair bit of cash anyway. A hawk cost as much as £5, an enormous amount, and a female peregrine, the most prized bird of all, far more. Many hunting birds were provided with privileged lives, living on luxurious perches in their master's room.
7. Borman.
8. Borman.
9. It did not become known as this for another century. In fact there were two books, the *Big Domesday* and *Little Domesday*, because East Anglia was a bit late in getting it sorted.
10. As Robert Tombs wrote, it showed England was a 'rich and developed agricultural country, with its forests already reduced to twentieth-century levels . . . and as much land under the plough as in 1900, using 650,000 oxen'.
11. In fact income tax was introduced in England as a temporary measure for the war with revolutionary France, and it's safe to say the threat from Napoleon is no longer a national security priority.
12. The Normans are also seen as being behind priestly celibacy, although this was just the way the world was going; in 1076 the Catholic Church banned priests from marrying, the main practical reason being to stop the Church being dominated by nepotism

and family corruption. The Normans just happened to turn up as this party was ending.

13. Morris.
14. Morris.
15. Ackroyd.
16. Tombs.
17. Tombs.
18. Tombs.

Chapter 11

1. Higham and Ryan.
2. Poole, A.L.
3. This is according to a dubious account by Orderic. Maybe William felt no guilt whatsoever.
4. http://www.marcmorris.org.uk/2013/09/the-death-of-william-conqueror-9 9.html
5. Barlow.
6. William of Malmesbury.
7. Anselm was also one of the greatest philosophers of the medieval Church, and the first to come up with the ontological argument for God, one that is deeply influential in philosophy and which is too complicated to get into here (i.e. I don't understand it).
8. Poole.
9. Bridgeford.
10. Poole.
11. Borman.
12. The spot where Rufus fell in the New Forest is today marked by the Rufus Stone, although this was only put up in the seventeenth century and it seems the authorities just picked a random place.

Chapter 12

1. Poole.

2. Most took the surname FitzRoy, Norman for 'son of a king'. Charles II is the only serious rival, with something like seventeen.

3. Queen Matilda was a great patron of learning, and of William of Malmesbury especially; Malmesbury, who had written all those critical things about the English, was actually half-Norman, half-English (like many writers this period) and was the first man since Bede to write a history of England, or at least a serious one that didn't depend on wizards and magic swords for explanations.

4. Poole, A.L.

5. Morris, Marc *King John*.

6. Castor, Helen.

7. Castor.

8. Asbridge, Thomas.

9. Matilda's father-in-law Fulk left immediately after the wedding to go to the Holy Land to try to worm his way into the affections of the heiress to the kingdom of Jerusalem. Unfortunately the rumor that she was having an affair with another crusader led to a civil war, until Fulk was eventually killed by falling from a horse.

10. For *Game of Thrones* fans, George RR Martin based King Joffrey's demise on this event, the 'Anarchy' being one inspiration for the War of the Five Kings.

Chapter 13

1. Ackroyd, Peter.

2. Ackroyd.

3. https://www.theguardian.com/education/2002/apr/13/artsandhumanities.highereducation1.

4. http://www.telegraph.co.uk/news/newstopics/howaboutthat/8424904/People-with-Norman-names-wealthier-than-other-Britons.html.

5. Stanton, Sir Frank.

6. http://www.caitlingreen.org/2015/05/medieval-new-england-black-sea.html.

7. According to historian Ian Mortimer between 80 and 95 percent of ethnically English people are descended from Edward III, and most likely closer to 100 percent. Tens of millions of Americans would also be.
8. Crystal, David.
9. Crystal.
10. Crystal.
11. Among the French words that entered in thirteenth century were *treasure, letter, cup, tribute, serve, marble, grace, abbey, nunnery* and *attire.*
12. Bridgeford.
13. Richard de Lucy, chief justiciar of England in the twelfth century..
14. Denzinger and Lacey.